A Guide to Gender-Analysis Frameworks

Candida March,
Ines Smyth, and
Maitrayee Mukhopadhyay

Oxfam

Contents

Acknowledgements

This book is based on an earlier pack compiled by Candida March for internal Oxfam use, which, in turn, built on the work of Maia Pinto and Sue Smith. The development of the pack was supported and managed by Maitrayee Mukhopadhyay. For the book, Ines Smyth has written an Introduction, placing the frameworks in the wider context of gender and development work.

The reason for producing the book (and the earlier pack) is to provide a single volume which discusses the most well-known gender analysis frameworks for development research and planning, with commentaries from users of each framework. The commentaries are based primarily on the experience of Oxfam staff members throughout the world, and their colleagues and associates in gender training networks and academic establishments. In addition, they owe much to work first presented in *Reversed Realities* by Naila Kabeer, Verso, 1994.

In its discussion of the various gender frameworks and how they are used, the book draws substantially on ideas, and words, from many other publications, including Oxfam's own *Gender Training Manual*. Oxfam is grateful to all the individuals and organisations whose work appears here for permission to use their material, and wherever possible, the source is acknowledged in the appropriate places in the text. In addition, the sources reappear in the bibliography at the end of the book. We would be glad to hear from anyone whose material has not been fully acknowledged, so that any omissions can be corrected should the book be reprinted.

Finally, the book owes much to Elsa Dawson, Judy El Bushra, Sukey Field, Laurie Forcier, Georgia Gill, Karoline Kuprat, Yvonne Kuprat, Margaret Legum, Nazneen Kanji, Caren Levy, Fra von Massow, Debbie Mander, Dorinne Plantenga, Tahmina Rahman, Mohga Kamal Smith, and Caroline Sweetman.

1 | The context of this book

1.1 | Introduction

Ines Smyth

This short guide to gender-analysis tools and gender frameworks is based on a pack developed in 1996 for the use of Oxfam staff and partners. The book aims to be a stand-alone resource, discussing the methodologies of the best known analytical frameworks which have been used to integrate gender considerations into development initiatives. It gives practical examples of each framework, and provides accessible commentaries discussing the frameworks' potential uses, advantages, and limitations, as well as recent adaptations. The commentaries draw on a wide range of experience of Oxfam staff, partners, and colleagues in other organisations, who have used the gender frameworks in various training, planning, and evaluation processes throughout the world.

The book is intended to meet the needs of development practitioners, trainers, researchers, and students for an introduction to such gender frameworks; we hope that, in addition, it will be of use to those who are already familiar with the main concepts and methodologies. However, this guide does not seek to be a comprehensive manual or a rigorous teaching text; for example, it does not cover the wide range of techniques and information contained in the original gender frameworks. Most importantly, the users' commentaries are not exhaustive, nor have they been collated in a 'scientific' way. They simply capture some experiences of gender and development workers in using the frameworks, and outline the possibilities and constraints of working with different gender frameworks in particular contexts. The book is intended as a 'taster', providing readers with a glimpse of the many practical insights that such gender frameworks can offer.

We hope that this will stimulate readers to turn to the texts where the gender frameworks are set out in more detail. Those who are not in a position to apply the gender frameworks in direct and immediate ways – managers of development organisations and government agencies, researchers, students, and trainers – can all benefit from the insights that the original texts offer, and from the deep commitment to gender equity in which they are rooted.

Before we introduce and discuss the selected gender frameworks, this introduction intends to locate them in the broader context of integrating gender considerations into development work. We wish to emphasise that using gender-analysis frameworks can encourage a practice of development which has the potential to contribute to the struggle for gender equality and for women's rights. However, such a potential can be realised only if appropriate gender frameworks are used and applied in a sensitive and skilled manner. Moreover, their use must be based on a political, and personal, commitment to a principle of social justice which includes gender equity.

The history of gender concerns in development organisations

A concern for gender equality in development is sufficiently well established to be the subject of historical accounts. Such accounts often describe an evolution in development policy and planning from a so-called welfare approach, to one which prioritised equity, then efficiency, and finally to one which espouses women's empowerment as its goal (Moser 1993). Such approaches are also seen to coexist, either as single policies of a particular government or agency, or mixed-and-matched within one organisation, in the hope that they will form a coherent whole (Andersen 1992).

Whatever the merit of such accounts, the most important distinction they make is that between two policy perspectives: WID (Women in Development), which aims to include women in development projects in order to make them more efficient, and GAD (Gender and Development), which addresses inequalities in women's and men's social roles in relation to development. The advantages of the shift which has supposedly taken place from one to the other have been amply discussed elsewhere (for example, Elson 1995 and Kabeer 1994), and need not be further described here. The point is that even within GAD, a variety of perspectives coexist (Levy 1996). As a consequence, GAD as a policy and planning approach remains complex, both in terms of language and in terms of the possible practices which it encompasses.

Something else appears from the historical accounts of the different inter-pretations of women and gender issues in development. From the earlier debates it was clear that societal attitudes are pervasive: thus they influence the nature of projects intended for women and their ability to achieve their objectives (Buvinic 1984). With the shift from WID to GAD, this realisation came into sharper focus: development bureaucracies and other related organisations were seen to be 'gendered', in terms of their culture, rules and outcomes (Goetz 1995). In patriarchal societies, this means that the organisations' culture, rules, and outcomes are modelled on male values and attitudes. Thus, they are often inimical to women, fail to recognise and reward their contributions to the organisation, and therefore recreate and reproduce the gender hierarchies and inequalities dominant in the wider world.

What is 'mainstreaming' gender?

Turning one's attention from what development actors do, and what approach they use, to who they are, leads to the call for organisations to 'mainstream' gender – to integrate gender concerns into every aspect of an organisation's priorities and procedures. The precise meaning of 'mainstreaming' as an aim, and the ways in which this can occur, are contested terrain. For many, 'mainstreaming' means making gender concerns the responsibility of all in an organisation, and ensuring that they are integrated into all structures and all work. (This is seen as an alternative to making gender concerns the sole responsibility of a smaller specialist team or unit.) Critics of this approach have pointed out the disadvantages of trying to achieve the goal of 'mainstreaming' gender by making it everyone's responsibility. They argue that this may lead to diluting or distorting these issues, or making them disappear altogether, as a result of lack of consistent attention and resources, sustained commitment on the part of decision-makers, and of male resistance. In contrast, it is argued that a specialist team, although it may be working in the 'margins', may oblige organisations to develop and maintain a more visible and radical commitment to gender equality.

Confusingly, others use a different approach in trying to achieve 'mainstreaming': one which separates out the systems and tasks necessary to address gender concerns, by establishing national 'machineries' or specialist teams (such as ministries, special units, and so on). This has been a way in which governments and organisations can signal their acknowledgement of the importance of women's issues (del Rosario 1995). Yet this approach, too, has been found wanting. In particular, national machineries have often been 'proven to be weak, under-resourced, vulnerable to changing political fortunes and to co-optation by political parties' (Byrne and Laire 1996, 1).

The current consensus seems to be that organisations need to use both approaches – integrating gender concerns throughout the organisation, as well as maintaining specialist departments or units – in order to avoid marginalisation and co-optation of gender issues. In general, 'mainstreaming' is understood as a welcome departure from an 'integrationist' approach, which is simply concerned with allowing women access to development activities and bureaucracies. 'Mainstreaming gender is both a technical and political process which requires shifts in organisational cultures and ways of thinking, as well as in the goals, structures, and resources allocation of international agencies, government, and NGOs.' (Kardam 1998)[1]

The role of gender-analysis frameworks in 'mainstreaming' gender

From the early debates, gender analysts have agreed that 'mainstreaming' gender into our organisational culture, structures, and work necessitates not only understanding what this goal should be, but also how it can be achieved

(Buvinic 1984, Andersen 1992). The need for practical instruments has been expressed by policy makers and by those who implement development programmes and projects at different levels. For example, Caroline Moser stressed that '...many of those committed to integrating gender into their work at policy, programme, and project levels still lack the necessary planning principles and methodological tools... planners require simplified tools which allow them to feed the particular complexities of specific contexts into the planning process'. (Moser 1993, 5)

According to Maya Buvinic, the task of 'mainstreaming' gender in organisations, using both approaches, means that attention must be paid to three issues:

- the internal and external political processes in which a particular development organisation and its members may be engaged;

- the setting up of the so-called 'machineries', entrusted with the task of incorporating women and/or gender issues into the design and implementation of policies;

- the development of appropriate 'tools and technical capabilities'. (Buvinic 1984, 21)

This book focuses on the third of these components, that of 'tools and technical capabilities' or, more specifically, gender frameworks.

What is meant by 'gender frameworks' in this book? In theory and practice, three terms are often used interchangeably: methodology, framework, and tools. This language is inherited from the tradition of academic research, which uses the term 'methodology' to refer to the combination of theories, concepts, and selected 'observation techniques' (Pelto and Pelto 1990; Mikkelsen 1995). In this context, the words 'methodology' and 'framework' are often used interchangeably, and 'tools' are discussed as components of methodologies. Tools would include observation techniques such as participant observation, the wide range of Participatory Rural Appraisal (PRA) techniques, or the more formal surveys which provide quantitative data.

In this book, we have chosen to use the term 'framework' to mean 'methods of research and planning for assessing and promoting gender issues in institutions'.[2] This is for two reasons. First, this seems to be the most common usage of the term among trainers and development practitioners, and therefore those most interested will easily recognise it. Second, it seems more appropriate to reserve the use of the word 'tool' for those observation and other research techniques (participatory or not) which users of gender frameworks employ.

By collecting, explaining, and illustrating a number of well-known gender frameworks commonly used in development work, this book tries to respond to a demand for practical instruments. We aim to make the main gender frameworks, and feedback from those who have used them, available to a broad constituency of practitioners and scholars in development. Although it is not intended as a manual or a teaching text, the book also tries to mediate some of the complexities inherent in the understanding and the use of gender concepts and instruments.

The development of this Guide

Oxfam's own attempts at a full and genuine integration of gender into its 'vision' and its work, and its difficulties and achievements, have been documented elsewhere (Porter, Smyth, and Sweetman 1999, Macdonald 1994, Wallace and March 1991). The demand for 'practical instruments' has been a common one within Oxfam, voiced by people in different roles and locations.

In developing the original pack in 1996, Oxfam never intended to provide a comprehensive commentary from users on all available gender frameworks, and on the practical integration of a gender perspective into planning. Planning methods and instruments of this type often remain accessible only to some individuals and their organisations, either because they are considered their 'intellectual property', or simply because opportunities have not arisen to share and disseminate them more widely. Thus, the pack limited itself to discussing those gender frameworks which were best known to Oxfam at the time, and to providing a 'user commentary' of each, drawing on the experience of Oxfam staff, partners, and like-minded organisations. The pack was widely distributed and used both inside and outside Oxfam, and we were told that it was an extremely useful document. As a result, it was decided that the pack deserved to be widely disseminated, as an official publication.

Regarding the choice of the gender frameworks included, both in the pack and now in the book, we have maintained the limited scope of the original pack, partly to retain the easily accessible nature of the publication, and partly because those consulted expressed little interest in a broader coverage. In all probability, we have therefore excluded less well known or readily available, but equally useful, gender frameworks, including many which have been developed for use in specific sectors such as health, and many which have been developed in the South (where opportunities for exposure through publishing and other means of dissemination may be limited). The Guide also does not include a thorough account of the many adaptations of existing gender frameworks which have been made by research institutions, governments, and others to reflect different contexts and priorities. (The exception is the Moser Framework, which has undergone considerable developments, some of which are reflected here.)

Finally, most of the gender frameworks included in this Guide are narrowly applicable to programmes and projects, and therefore difficult to broaden out and apply to the social or organisational contexts. The exceptions are the DPU

Framework (an adaptation of the Moser Framework), and the Social Relations Approach, both of which provide the possibility for institutional analysis.

We have had the opportunity to develop and update the original pack by including additional ideas and experiences of development practitioners and gender trainers who have used the gender frameworks and the pack itself. We sent a questionnaire to Oxfam staff, consultants, and other individuals in development and academic institutions, in the UK and beyond. Although not all the details of every response could be included (or publicly acknowledged), the comments have been used to revise the original commentaries from users, and, more generally, to inform the book's approach.

Several interesting points have emerged from this process of 'pre-testing' the book. The popularity of the original pack confirmed that the gender frameworks had generated a tremendous amount of interest among researchers and practitioners. Users of the pack confirmed that the manual was useful, with comments such as: 'Excellent booklet, very useful and a good design'; 'You really have covered the difficulties very comprehensively and concisely in this manual'; and 'Great training reference manual'. The popularity of the earlier document is also demonstrated by the fact that it has been translated in French, Spanish, Portuguese, Russian, and Arabic. The translations have served a dual purpose: they allow the gender frameworks to be used much more easily in work and training in different countries, and they make them more accessible to partner organisations.

We also noted that more replies and comments were sent back by trainers and researchers than by project and programme officers and other development workers. This may be simply as a result of ease of communication. It may also be a reflection of the fact that many people still do not feel confident enough in their knowledge of gender issues, and in their understanding of the concepts informing the gender frameworks. For some people, the available gender frameworks may be difficult to employ, and the rationale for their use may not be clear; in addition, the information on which the frameworks rely may be unavailable, while resource constraints may make thorough research impossible. Some of the replies which we received confirmed these considerations, and encouraged us that the publication of this book was a timely initiative.

Beyond gender frameworks to commitment

Despite its limited scope, this book responds to a felt and voiced need among practitioners and scholars of development for whom gender equality is a goal. But how far can these gender frameworks go towards achieving such a goal? Mainstreaming gender concerns is a political endeavour within institutions, because the process challenges existing allocations of authority and resources, as well as cultural norms (Razavi and Miller 1995; Moser 1993, 109). Development organisations are often uncomfortable with such a 'radical' agenda, and especially uncomfortable with the language and aims of feminism. For a long time, such agencies have been decrying the lack of expertise and methodologies that prevents them from achieving their objectives. But they fail to acknowledge that their poor results in redressing gender imbalances and injustices are due to ' the disparities in power and resources and conflict of interests' (Jahan 1995, 126) inside their own organisations. Clarity about their gender-specific objectives and strategies is essential to clarify the 'why' and what an individual organisation is trying to achieve, before they can make informed choice on the 'how', in terms of the methodologies they promote.

As has been stated above, the explanation of how to apply each framework is accompanied by a brief commentary from users. These individual commentaries should go some way in alerting readers and prospective users that there are potential pitfalls, as well as gains, in employing such gender frameworks. However, it is also important to offer some more general warnings.

First, practitioners must be careful to employ gender frameworks in a serious, systematic way. Adequate resources, including time, skills, and suitable preparation, are all essential. Using the gender frameworks should go hand-in-hand with a coherent and gender-sensitive use of other relevant techniques, such as data collection. As Naila Kabeer says: 'No set of methods are in themselves sensitive to differences and inequalities between men and women; each method is only as good as its practitioner' (Kabeer 1995, 112).

Second, it is important to understand the limits of the frameworks in bringing about change. Development practitioners may see them as a simple way of 'doing gender', without the change in attitude which the realisation of the nature and importance of gender inequalities in development brings. Gender frameworks are a means to a bigger end: that of devising and implementing policies and programmes which do not exclude or harm women, which take their needs and perspective into account, and which may help redress some of the existing gender imbalances.

Those using gender frameworks must not ignore cultural difference. As Ruth Pearson points out: 'Gender planning frameworks are seductively universal, presented as providing universally applicable tools. Experience has shown, however, that they are not universal.' (ODA 1996). For instance, translating the key terms used in the gender frameworks presents considerable difficulties. Similarly, when the gender frameworks are used for training purposes, the trainer faces the considerable challenge of finding examples and case studies which reflect the realities of the individual location, in order to make the frameworks pertinent and effective. The negative consequence of an unquestioning approach can be that some of the beneficiaries of projects – or trainees, for example – are confused and offended by what they may perceive as insensitive attacks against their culture or personal life.

Finally, readers should be aware of what Kabeer (1994) calls the 'project trap'. The usefulness of the gender frameworks contained in this book is undisputed. However, with the exceptions mentioned earlier, they may encourage an exclusive focus on gender issues in development projects. This, in turn, can lead to practitioners ignoring the fact that gender equality must be fought for at other levels and by other means, for example through advocacy and the collective action of women. Women's organisations and groups, whether they call themselves 'feminist' or not, have been created to foster women's collective action against gender inequality. Their existence does not exonerate development organisations from exploring other means of tackling gender inequalities which go beyond and above the 'project trap'.

In part, the problems outlined above result from the widespread tendency of development practitioners to by-pass theory – in this case theories of gender and gender relations – in the mistaken assumption that a knowledge of 'facts' is sufficient for development work. Such problems are, above all, the result of seeing gender frameworks as purely technocratic tools, deprived of their political dimension. Techniques such as the gender frameworks which are the subject of this book can be political instruments – if they are used with the objective of addressing gender inequality. To deprive them of this rationale is to render them sterile and tokenistic 'tools', useful to make superficial adjustments rather than profound, long-lasting transformations.

This book urges caution, but it also celebrates the usefulness and potential of the gender frameworks which have been included. They represent the distillation of much knowledge and experience, of those who have developed them, those who have used them, and those who have been exposed to them. Employing, adapting, and developing such gender frameworks can represent a contribution to the overall goal of gender equity in development. We invite all readers and users of this guide to send their own comments to us at Oxfam GB, for inclusion in any future revised edition.

References

Andersen C (1992) 'Practical Guidelines', in Ostergaard L (ed.) *Gender and Development: A Practical Guide*, Routledge, London.

Buvinic M (1984) 'Project for Women in the Third World: Explaining their Misbehaviour', International Centre for Research on Women, Washington.

Byrne B and Laire JK (1996) 'National Machineries for Women in Development: Experiences, Lessons and Strategies for Institutionalising Gender in Development Policy and Planning', Bridge Report 35, IDS, University of Sussex.

del Rosario V (1995) 'Mainstreaming Gender Concerns: Aspects of Compliance Resistance and Negotiation', in *IDS Bulletin 26:3, Getting*

Institutions Right for Women in Development, University of Sussex.

Elson D (ed) (1995) *Male Bias in the Development Process*, Manchester University Press, Manchester.

Jahan R (1995) *The Elusive Agenda: Mainstreaming Women in Development*, Zed Books, London.

Kabeer N (1994) *Reversed Realities*, Verso, London.

Kabeer N (1995) 'Targeting women or transforming institutions? Policy lessons from NGOs' anti-poverty efforts', in *Development in Practice 5:2*, Oxfam GB, Oxford.

Kardam N (1998) 'Changing Institutions in Women's Interests', in *Development and Gender In Brief 5*.

Goetz AM (1995) 'Institutionalising Women's Interests and Gender-Sensitive Accountability in Development' in *IDS Bulletin 26:3, Getting Institutions Right For Women in Development*, University of Sussex.

Levy C (1996) 'The Process of Institutionalising Gender in Policy and Planning: The "Web" of Institutionalisation', Working Paper No. 74, Development Planning Unit, University College London.

Macdonald M (1994) *Gender Planning in Development Agencies*, Oxfam GB, Oxford.

March C (1996) 'A Tool Kit: Concepts and Frameworks for Gender Analysis and Planning', unpublished internal document, Oxfam GB, Oxford.

Mikkelsen B (1995) *Methods for Development Work and Research*, Sage Publications, London.

Moser C (1993), *Gender Planning and Development :Theory, Practice and Training*, Routledge, London.

ODA (1996) 'Towards the design of a post-Beijing Training Strategy', workshop report.

Pelto P and Pelto G (1970) *Anthropological Research*, Cambridge University Press, Cambridge.

Porter F, Smyth I, Sweetman C (eds.) (1999) *Gender Works*, Oxfam GB, Oxford.

Razavi S and Miller C (1995) *Gender Mainstreaming*, UNRISD, Geneva.

Wallace T and March C (1991) *Changing Perceptions*, Oxfam GB, Oxford.

1.2 | Key concepts

The practical use of gender-analysis frameworks must be based on the clear understanding of their central concepts. The concepts can also be used in research and planning, independently of the gender frameworks.

All explanations and definitions given need to be translated and adapted to each local context. While all of the concepts here may be of use in your area of work, only a few of them are essential in all situations. For example, it would be impossible to perform a gender analysis without understanding the concepts of sex and gender, or how the division of labour between women and men is affected by, and in turn shapes, gender power relations. But some other concepts which are widely used – for example, practical and strategic gender needs – are not vital to do good work. They may even mislead, because reality does not fit into such neat categories. Use these concepts as a way to start thinking about the issues, but do not be intimidated by them, and only use what seems helpful to you in your work.

Terms and concepts included here are the subject of widespread and continuing debates by researchers and workers in academia and development organisations. We do not aim here to do justice to these complex debates; rather, we explain the terms and concepts briefly, as they are currently understood and used by gender and development practitioners.

Sex and Gender

The distinction between sex and gender is the subject of much discussion. In gender and development, definitions can be summarised as follows:

Sex: Sex is the biological difference between men and women. Sex differences are concerned with men's and women's bodies. Men produce sperm; women bear and breastfeed children. Sexual differences are the same throughout the human race.

Gender: Sex is a fact of human biology; gender is not. The experience of being male or female differs dramatically from culture to culture. The concept of gender[3] is used by sociologists to describe all the socially given attributes, roles, activities, and responsibilities connected to being a male or a female in a given society. Our gender identity determines how we are perceived, and how we are expected to think and act as women and men, because of the way society is organised.

Gender relations: These are the social relationships between men as a sex and women as a sex. Gender relations are simultaneously relations of co-operation, connection, and mutual support, and of conflict, separation, and competition, of difference and inequality. Gender relations are concerned with how power is distributed between the sexes. They create and reproduce systemic differences in men's and women's positions in a given society. They define the way in which responsibilities and claims are allocated and the way in which each is given a value. Gender relations vary according to time and place, and between different groups of people. They also vary according to other social relations such as class, race, ethnicity, disability, and so on.

Gender analysis: Such an analysis explores and highlights the relationships of women and men in society, and the inequalities in those relationships, by asking: Who does what? Who has what? Who decides? How? Who gains? Who loses? When we pose these questions, we also ask: Which men? Which women? Gender analysis breaks down the divide between the private sphere (involving personal relationships) and the public sphere (which deals with relationships in wider society). It looks at how power relations within the household interrelate with those at the international, state, market, and community level.

Gender and development work is based on gender analysis. This involves promoting equality between men and women; key to this is placing the issues that women say are of particular concern to them on the main agenda of those institutions which shape women's and men's lives (the state, non-government organisations, and so on).

Work

Gender (or sexual) division of labour

In all societies, men and women are assigned tasks, activities and responsibilities according to their sex. The gender division of labour varies from one society and culture to another, and within each culture, it also changes with external circumstances and over time. Because in most societies, gender power relations are skewed in favour of men, different values are ascribed to men's tasks and women's tasks.

In all types of work done by men and women, a distinction can be made between productive work (production) and reproductive work (reproduction).

Production: This includes the production of goods and services for income or subsistence. It is this work which is mainly recognised and valued as work by individuals and societies, and which is most commonly included in national economic statistics. Both women and men perform productive work, but not all of this is valued or rewarded in the same way.

Reproduction: This encompasses the care and maintenance of the household and its members, such as cooking, washing, cleaning, nursing, bearing children and looking after them, building and maintaining shelter. This work is necessary, yet it is rarely considered of the same value as productive work. It is normally unpaid and is not counted in conventional economic statistics. It is mostly done by women.

Access to, and control over, resources

When considering the way in which resources are allocated between women and men (the 'gendered' allocation of resources), it is important to look at the difference between access to resources and control over them.

Access: This is defined as the opportunity to make use of a resource.

Control: This is the power to decide how a resource is used, and who has access to it.

Women often have access but no control.

Status and role

There are a number of different sets of concepts which aim to distinguish between the visible aspects of gender relations between women and men (for example, as seen in the different activities they participate in), and the invisible power relations which determine these activities. As a result of their low status in the community, the activities which women perform tend to be valued less than men's; and in turn, women's low status is perpetuated through the low value placed on their activities.

Condition and position

Condition: This term describes the immediate, material circumstances in which men and women live, related to their present workloads and responsibilities. Providing clean water or stoves for cooking, for example, may improve the condition of women by reducing their workload.

Position: This concept describes the place of women in society relative to that of men. Changing women's position requires addressing their strategic gender interests (see below for a full definition of this term), including equal access to decision-making and resources, getting rid of discrimination in employment, land ownership, and so on. In order to change women's position, we must address the way gender determines power, status, and control over resources.

Practical and strategic gender interests/ needs[4]

The dual concept of women's – or men's – practical and strategic gender interests (first coined by Maxine Molyneux in 1985) was developed into a tool for planners by Caroline Moser (see p 55 for the Moser Framework), which looks at 'needs' rather than interests.

Practical gender interests/ needs: If these were met, the lives of women (or men) would be improved without changing the existing gender division of labour or challenging women's subordinate position in society. Meeting practical interests/ needs is a response to an immediate perceived necessity; interventions which do this are typically concerned with inadequacies in living conditions such as water provision, health care, and employment.

Strategic gender interests/ needs: If these were met, the existing relationship of unequal power between men and women would be transformed. These interests/ needs relate to gender divisions of labour, power, and control. Those identified by women may include issues such as legal rights, domestic violence, equal wages, and women's control over their bodies. However, many of these issues are perceived as part of a natural order, which cannot be challenged. Women may only be able to articulate their strategic interests/ needs once they have exchanged knowledge with someone who knows that it is possible to change the 'natural order'. This may be an external facilitator, or a community member who has experienced another environment or culture (for example, a returning migrant worker). Men also have strategic interests/ needs: they may aim to transform their own roles (in order to be able to take part in child-care or to resist conscription into a fighting force), or, on the other hand, they may resist women's demands for more control over their own lives.

Some have argued that practical and strategic interests and needs cannot be so neatly separated. Sara Longwe points out that every practical development intervention has an effect on power relations (the 'strategic' area of life), whether this is intended or not.

Transformatory (or redistributive) potential

Kate Young (1987) introduced a concept of transformatory potential, to complement the concepts of practical needs and strategic gender interests (Young's chosen terminology). This is a useful concept to help development planners, or women themselves, to consider how their practical needs can be met in a way which has transformatory potential; that is, in a way which will assist women in challenging unequal gender power relations, and contribute to women's empowerment.

Gender classifications of policies

As a tool for helping practitioners and policy-makers determine to what degree a project or a policy is explicitly working towards transforming unequal gender relations, Naila Kabeer (1992) classifies policies into the following types.

Gender-blind policies: These recognise no distinction between the sexes. They make assumptions, which leads to a bias in favour of existing gender relations. Therefore, gender-blind policies tend to exclude women.

Gender-aware policies: This type of policy recognises that women are development actors as well as men; that the nature of women's involvement is determined by gender relations which make their involvement different, and often unequal; and that consequently women may have different needs, interests, and priorities which may sometimes conflict with those of men. Within this category, Kabeer further distinguishes between gender-neutral, gender-specific, and gender-redistributive policies.

Gender-neutral policies use the knowledge of gender differences in a given society to overcome biases in development interventions, in order to ensure that interventions target and benefit both sexes effectively to meet their practical gender needs. Gender-neutral policies work within the existing gender division of resources and responsibilities.

Gender-specific policies use the knowledge of gender differences in a given context to respond to the practical gender needs of women or men; they work within the existing gender division of resources and responsibilities.

Gender-redistributive policies are intended to transform existing distributions of power and resources to create a more balanced relationship between women and men, touching on strategic gender interests. They may target both sexes, or women or men separately.

1.3 | Choosing a framework

The choice of a suitable framework will depend on the task in hand, the context, and the resources available. This section discusses some of the issues involved, and aims to achieve easy comparison and choice. There are many similarities between the different gender-analysis frameworks: for example, all of them recognise and emphasise the existence of reproductive work alongside productive activities. However, despite the many similarities, the gender frameworks differ in their scope and emphasis.

You do not necessarily need a formal framework in order to work well or innovatively on gender issues, to reduce gender inequality, or to support women's empowerment. These frameworks are practical instruments, designed to help their users integrate a gender analysis into social research and planning. If you are committed to bringing about change, using a framework may take you one step further towards understanding the issues, facts, and relationships which affect women's and men's lives in a given society. Gender frameworks are useful if they help you think through your own way of planning and doing things; they will not be useful if you find them confusing, too bureaucratic, or restrictive. Also, it is essential to remember that no framework will do the work for you. It may help you plan the work that can be done to confront women's subordination. Afterwards, the work must still be done.

Because a framework selects a limited number of factors as important, out of the huge numbers of issues that actually influence on any situation, each framework can only produce a crude model of reality. The selection of factors in any particular framework reflects a set of values and assumptions on the part of the author(s) of the framework. You yourself also have a set of values and assumptions. The interplay between these two sets of values and assumptions will determine which approaches and interventions you consider, and which you select.

You can also combine gender frameworks designed by others to create your own hybrid version, adapting different components of separate gender frameworks and adding your own ideas. In fact, many of the frameworks included here have been developed in such a way, for example, the Harvard Framework and People-Oriented Planning (POP). Some frameworks use similar concepts, such as the Harvard Framework and the Moser Framework. Finally, some concepts which are part of a more complicated framework can actually be used by themselves in a fruitful way.

Comparing gender frameworks

When selecting a framework for your particular work, it is important to consider their main conceptual differences. in the following, we have listed the most useful questions to ask.

To what extent does the framework incorporate an analysis of social relations which goes beyond issues of gender?

Gender relations are context-specific; they vary considerably depending on the setting. They are shaped by other aspects of relationships between people, including economic status, race, ethnicity, or disability. All these social categories play a part in determining an individual's power and status in their particular community. So, for instance, in any village gender relations will differ between the richest and the poorest community members.

How flexible are different gender frameworks?

Given time, gender roles and relations change naturally in any community. Sometimes, specific events such as conflict or economic crisis cause certain aspects to change rapidly or dramatically. In order to identify opportunities and constraints for working towards greater gender equity, development workers must be able to recognise both actual and potential changes in gender relations. No gender analysis can be static; it must recognise that change over time will occur, and examine how this will affect the society, and thus the project or programme. The Harvard Framework and the Longwe Framework in particular do not automatically include time as a variable; in contrast, the People-Oriented Planning (POP) Framework and the Social Relations Approach are centred on change over time.

Does the framework mainly analyse social roles or social relations?

A gender analysis which focuses primarily on roles takes as its starting point the gender division of labour, and the gendered distribution of resources. A gender-roles analysis therefore sees a community mainly in terms of who does what, who has what, and so on. Alternatively, a gender analysis which focuses on relations sees a community mainly in terms of how members relate to each other: what bargains they make, what bargaining power they have, what they get in return; when they act with self-interest, when they act altruistically, and so on. The Harvard Analytical Framework can be considered a method of gender-roles analysis, whereas the Social Relations Approach is a method of gender-relations analysis.

Both roles and relations are important. However, the analytical gender frameworks which focus on roles, such as the Harvard Framework, may encourage users to think of men and women as separate groups, as if they could be isolated from each other. If you use a roles analysis, you may end up dissecting gender relations rather than creating a picture of the different ways in which everything, conflicts as well as co-operation between men and women, fits together. Naila Kabeer (1992) points out that, in particular, a gender-roles analysis does not directly examine how power is structured and negotiated (see also the users' commentaries of the Harvard and POP frameworks on pp 48-54). In contrast, gender frameworks which focus on relations, such as the Social Relations Approach, attempt to reverse this trend by first of all analysing the relationship between people: relationships of power related to class, race, age, and so on, and, of course, gender.

A fairly crude analogy of the difference between these two approaches is that of a machine. An analysis which focuses on roles takes the machine to pieces, and describes the components and how each component works. An analysis which focuses on relations draws a map or a diagram of how all the components work in relation to each other. (The Moser Framework falls somewhere in between these. The concept of roles is central to Moser's analysis, but she emphasises that roles need to be seen clearly in the context of the relations between men and women.)

A fish-smoking project developed by UNIFEM in Guinea illustrates the dangers of using a gender-roles analysis only. A gender-roles analysis, similar to the Harvard Framework, revealed the following division of labour: men caught fish; women smoked and sold the fish. The project formed the women into groups and introduced new improved stoves.

However, the project failed, because no thought had been given to how the women got the fish. Women usually got their fish through special relationships of mutual advantage with specific fishermen. When the project started, the women were seen to be beneficiaries of external funds and the fishermen increased their prices. The women could not afford to buy at the increased prices, either as individuals or as groups.

A working system had been disrupted and no viable alternative put in its stead. A relations analysis would have looked closely at the relationships between the men and the women and tried to start from there.[5]

How much does each framework include and value intangible, as well as tangible, resources?

Intangible resources include political or social resources: rights and claims on people; friendships; membership of networks; skills; experience of working in the public sphere; self-confidence and credibility; status and respect; leadership qualities; and, often crucially for women, time. If people have very few tangible resources such as land or income, intangible resources are especially important in shaping their lives. The extent to which the different gender frameworks include and value intangible resources varies, but the Harvard Framework has a particularly narrow definition of resources.

What is the ultimate goal of each framework? Is it focusing on efficiency or empowerment?

Gender-analysis frameworks concentrate on certain factors in women's and men's lives. The chosen focus reflects a set of values and assumptions on the part of the framework's designers. When you use a framework, these values and assumptions will ultimately influence the type of development interventions you select. It is important, therefore, to be aware, as far as possible, of the thinking behind the gender frameworks.

The efficiency approach to women in development (WID, see p 9) is based on the understanding that it is inefficient to ignore women in planning a distribution of resources. It aims to create projects and programmes with the most efficient allocation of resources. (This approach lies behind the Harvard and POP frameworks.) Although this approach seems very sensible, there are times when it can come into conflict with wider issues of justice or women's empowerment. As a consequence, the efficiency approach has been heavily criticised as follows. First, it does not challenge existing gender relations, and so tends to lead to gender-neutral or gender-specific policies or interventions. Because resources, not power, are seen as central, it can also further tip the balance of power in the favour of men. For example, further resources will be allocated to men if it is judged efficient, even if this is to the detriment of women. Similarly, if it does not make a project more efficient to involve women then, following the logic of the efficiency argument you should not do so, and ignore issues of justice. This approach can be particularly problematic in countries where women are not involved in production outside the house (see Harvard and POP commentaries on pp 48-54). But gender relations are complex; there is more at stake than just economics.

Other gender frameworks explicitly have the aim of empowerment. These emphasise the transformation of gender relations, through women's self-empowerment. 'Because there are risks and costs incurred in any process of change, such change must be believed in, initiated, and directed by those whose interests it is meant to serve. Empowerment cannot be given, it must be self-generated. All that a gender transformatory policy can hope to do is to provide women with the enabling resources which will allow them to take greater control of their own lives, to determine what kinds of gender relations they would want to live within, and to devise the strategies and alliances to help them get there' (Kabeer, 1994, 97).

(For more detail on different policy aims of gender-focused projects and programmes, see the Moser Framework, p 55.)

Of course it is perfectly possible to use the gender frameworks (or parts of them) in ways which subvert their stated goals. For example, the Moser Framework could be used to design projects which address women's practical gender needs only, with no attempt to support women's self-empowerment.

What is the role of the planner in the framework?

Implicit in each framework is the planner's own view of his or her role, which can range from benign top-down planner to the planner as facilitator only. One gender framework – the Social Relations Approach – explicitly requires the planners to examine their own institutions and understand how the institutions bring biases into the planning process.

Which gender frameworks can also be used in work addressing male gender identity and roles?

In practice, gender-analysis frameworks do not tend to be used to plan interventions which target men or boys. However, a gender analysis should take place for all interventions, because they all have a potential impact on gender relations, and therefore on both sexes.

Furthermore, understanding gender relations is critical to understanding possibilities and constraints for working with men only. It is particularly critical to understand the 'gendered' nature of men in societies where gender roles are changing rapidly. There is an increasing awareness that gender identity cross-cuts other identity issues, including race and class, to affect men's and women's roles in the gender division of labour. Development organisations need to address these issues in the context of work with ex-combatants, in areas of mass male unemployment, in anti-violence projects, among migrant workers, and so on.

Most of the gender frameworks – except the Women's Empowerment (Longwe) Framework – do look at the gender roles and relations of both women and men, and so could be used for projects which target men. The Moser Framework looks at the strategic gender needs of women only, but the DPU's adaptation (see Appendix, p 123) includes men as well, and can also be used with projects which address male gender issues. The Gender Analysis Matrix (GAM) includes men as one of its four categories of analysis and can therefore be used for projects which target men.

Making your choice

Gender analysis frameworks have been designed for different purposes. These purposes include range from helping you carry out your initial research, planning and monitoring an intervention, to evaluating what it has achieved.

Context analysis: Frameworks give you a way of thinking about the context which shapes the relationships and dynamics of any situation or group.

Visualisation and planning: The framework's tools provide you with a way of representing key points in a simple manner, to aid decision-making.

Communications: The tools help you share information, train people or sensitise them to gender issues.

Monitoring and evaluation: Framework tools can highlight the strengths and weaknesses of a particular development intervention.

Gender frameworks have sometimes been designed for use in a particular context. For instance, if you are working in emergency situations, there are two gender frameworks specifically designed for this (the People-Oriented Planning Framework, and the Capacities and Vulnerabilities Framework).

When deciding which framework to use for any particular situation, it is important to consider what aspects are appropriate in your work, and what purpose you are trying to achieve. There are a number of considerations.

Does the framework do what I want it to do?

What are you trying to achieve? What resources do you have? In each commentary from users of individual gender frameworks, we have tried to highlight the main purposes, strengths, and weaknesses of each framework, as experienced by gender and development workers and trainers. These commentaries are not exhaustive – all readers are invited to add to it. However, they do aim to help you choose an appropriate framework for your particular purpose – for training, planning or evaluation; for use in community projects, or at a level beyond the community; for communities to use themselves, or for policy makers to employ.

What will people's reactions be?

What will people's reactions be to using the framework, and to the conclusions that it enables them to reach? Increasingly, it is understood that organisations involved in development work reflect the biases of their own cultures. This 'gendered' nature of organisations, as well as of the communities with whom they work, has a profound impact on the success or failure of any development intervention. It is therefore very important to consider the culture of the individuals or organisations you are working with, and how this affects their capacity to work on gender. Some organisations and individuals will be resistant to thinking of relationships between women and men as relations of power, and to the idea of working for women's empowerment. You will have to think carefully about how explicitly and openly you want to challenge such resistance, and you should consider which other strategies you can employ to introduce new ideas to people. Some gender frameworks are particularly helpful in analysing how organisations, and the people within them, interact with and react to the external situation and development interventions. In particular, the Social Relations Approach and the DPU's Web of Institutionalisation (see Appendix, p 123) will help you think about the links between power and resources, between the institutions which determine who receives resources, and the communities with whom they work.

Some of the gender frameworks have arisen from specific disciplines of work or research, and were originally designed for use by or on behalf of specific groups of people. These often expand on concepts and use language already familiar to those working in the discipline in order to make the framework more appealing to that group. Examples include the Harvard Analytical Framework and the Moser Framework, which use the language of policy makers and planners.

What are the potential limitations of the framework? How can these be taken into account and compensated for?

In some cases, the potential limitations of a framework will have a greater negative impact than in others. Some can be compensated for by using another tool. For example, the Longwe framework, which does not consider the gender interests and needs of men, could be accompanied by an analysis of gender power relations between women and men. However, if you have very little time to use a framework, a comprehensive framework such as the Social Relations Approach may seem too complex; despite its good points, you would have to take a pragmatic decision on its suitability.

2 | The gender-analysis frameworks and users' commentaries

2.1 | Explaining the chapters

This section gives an overview of how the rest of this book is structured. Each gender framework is discussed in its own chapter. Within the chapters, you will find the following headings.

Background

This brief introduction gives information on the framework's author(s), when the framework was devised, and in what context.

Aims of the framework

This section gives more detailed information on what purpose the original framework was intended to fulfil.

Framework

Under this heading, you will find a brief outline of the key concepts of the framework, and an account of how it is normally used.

Much of the material used in this and the next section are taken directly from published and unpublished material written by the intellectual author(s) of the framework, or from gender and development workers who have developed training materials on the framework. As far as is possible, all concerned have given permission for their ideas and words to be used, and full credits are given at the start of the chapter (also see Acknowledgements, p V).

Case study

For each framework, a short case study is presented. These are only examples to illustrate how the framework was applied in practice. They do not represent the best, or the only, way of using the framework. Depending on the context you are working in, and the type of planning you are undertaking, your way of using it may well be different. Moreover, each case study has been summarised. In practice, a great deal more detail would be needed for planning purposes.

Commentary

This section is the main contribution of this book to the literature on gender-analysis frameworks. The views in this section are the personal views of gender and development workers and trainers in North and South, some, but not all of whom, have worked with Oxfam GB.

Uses

This section outlines the main uses of the framework. Of course the gender frameworks could always be used in additional ways.

Why it appeals

This section gives the main reasons why gender and development workers and trainers like the framework, and what they consider its main strengths.

Potential limitations

Before choosing or using the framework, you should consider its weaknesses which other workers and trainers have found. These potential weaknesses do not invalidate the usefulness of the gender frameworks; but you should be aware of them. It has been left to you, the reader, to decide whether the limitations will be significant in your context, whether you will still use the framework, and, if so, how you can compensate for the limitations. Whenever users have reported adaptations of the gender frameworks which help to balance or counteract potential limitations, these are included in the text.

Further reading

Under this heading, you will find a list of literature by the frameworks' intellectual author(s).

2.2 | Harvard Analytical Framework and People-Oriented Planning

These two gender frameworks appear in the same section because People-Oriented Planning is based on the Harvard Analytical Framework. After the two frameworks are presented, a joint commentary from users follows, which discusses those features which both frameworks share. Thereafter, two separate sub-sections examine the distinctive features of each framework.

Harvard Analytical Framework

Background

The Harvard Analytical Framework is often referred to as the Gender Roles Framework or Gender Analysis Framework. Published in 1985, it was one of the first frameworks designed for gender analysis. It was developed by researchers at the Harvard Institute for International Development in the USA, working in collaboration with the WID office of USAID, at a time when the 'efficiency approach' to integrating women in development work was gaining prominence in development circles.

The information about the Harvard Analytical Framework given here comes from Overholt, Anderson, Austin, and Cloud (1985) *Gender Roles in Development Projects*, published by Kumarian Press Inc, Connecticut; a second edition has been published by Lynne Rienner Publishers.

Aims of the Framework

The Harvard Framework was designed to demonstrate that there is an economic case for allocating resources to women as well as men. The framework aims to help planners design more efficient projects and improve overall productivity. It does this by mapping the work and resources of men and women in a community and highlighting the main differences.

The framework

The Harvard Analytical Framework is a grid (also known as a matrix) for collecting data at the micro-level (i.e., at the community and household level). It is a useful way of organising information and can be adapted to many situations. The Harvard Analytical Framework has four main components.

Harvard Tool 1: The Activity Profile

This tool identifies all relevant productive and reproductive tasks and answers the question: who does what?

How much detail you need depends on the nature of your project. Those areas of activity which the project will be directly involved in require the greatest detail. For instance, an activity profile for an agricultural project would

Example of Harvard Tool 1: Activity profile		
Activities	Women/girls	Men/boys
Productive Activities		

Agriculture:
    activity 1
    activity 2, etc.		

Income generating:
    activity 1
    activity 2, etc.		

Employment:
    activity 1
    activity 2, etc.		

Other:		
Reproductive Activities		

Water related:
    activity 1
    activity 2, etc.		

Fuel related:		
Food preparation:		
Childcare:		
Health related:		
Cleaning and repair:		
Market related:		
Other:		

Adapted from: Overholt, Anderson, Cloud and Austin, Gender Roles in Development Projects, Kumarian Press Inc, Connecticut, 1985 (Source: Match 1991, 31)

list, according to the gender division of labour, each agricultural activity (such as land clearance, preparation, and so on) for each crop, or each type of field.

Depending on the context, other parameters may also be examined:

- Gender and age denominations: identifying whether adult women, adult men, their children, or the elderly carry out an activity;

- Time allocation: specifying what percentage of time is allocated to each activity, and whether it is carried out seasonally or daily;

- Activity locus: specifying where the activity is performed, in order to reveal people's mobility. Is work done at home, in the family field, the family shop, or elsewhere (within or beyond) the community?

Harvard Tool 2: The Access and Control Profile – resources and benefits

This tool enables users to list what resources people use to carry out the tasks identified in the Activity Profile. It indicates whether women or men have access to resources, who controls their use, and who controls the benefits of a household's (or a community's) use of resources. Access simply means that you are able to use a resource; but this says nothing about whether you have control over it. For example, women may have some access to local political processes but little influence or control over which issues are discussed and the final decisions. The person who controls a resource is the one ultimately able to make decisions about its use, including whether it can be sold.

Example of Harvard Tool 2: Access and control profile				
	Access		Control	
	Women	Men	Women	Men
Resources Land Equipment Labour Cash Education/training, etc. Other				
Benefits Outside income Asset ownership Basic needs (food, clothing, shelter etc) Education Political power/prestige Other				

Adapted from: Overholt, Anderson, Cloud and Austin, Gender Roles in Development Projects, Kumarian Press Inc, Connecticut, 1985 (Source: Match, 1991, 31)

Harvard Tool 3: Influencing factors

This tool allows you to chart factors which influence the differences in the gender division of labour, access, and control as listed in the two Profiles (Tools 1 and 2). Identifying past and present influences can give an indication of future trends. These factors must also be considered because they present opportunities and constraints to increasing the involvement of women in development projects and programmes.

Influencing factors include all those that shape gender relations, and determine different opportunities and constraints for men and women. These factors are far-reaching, broad, and interrelated. They include:

- community norms and social hierarchies, such as family/ community forms, cultural practices, and religious beliefs;

- demographic conditions;

- institutional structures, including the nature of government bureaucracies, and arrangements for the generation and dissemination of knowledge, skills, and technology;

- general economic conditions, such as poverty levels, inflation rates, income distribution, international terms of trade, and infrastructure;

- internal and external political events;

- legal parameters;

- training and education;

- attitude of community to development/assistance workers.

The purpose of identifying these influencing factors is to consider which ones affect women's or men's activities or resources, and how they, in turn,

Example of Harvard Tool 3: Influencing factors		
Influencing Factors	**Constraints**	**Opportunities**
• Community norms and social hierarchy • Demographic factors • Institutional structures • Economic factors • Political factors • Legal parameters • Training • Attitude of community to development workers		

Adapted from: Overholt, Anderson, Cloud and Austin, Gender Roles in Development Projects, Kumarian Press Inc, Connecticut, 1985 (Source: Match 1991, 31).

can affect them. This tool is intended to help you identify external constraints and opportunities which you should consider in planning your development interventions. It should help you anticipate what inputs will be needed to make the intervention successful from a gender perspective.

Harvard Tool 4: Checklist for Project-Cycle Analysis

This consists of a series of questions. They are designed to assist you to examine a project proposal or an area of intervention from a gender perspective, using gender-disaggregated data and capturing the different effects of social change on men and women.

Example of Harvard Tool 4: Checklist

The following set of questions are the key ones for each of the four main stages in the project cycle: identification, design, implementation, evaluation.

WOMEN'S DIMENSION IN PROJECT IDENTIFICATION
Assessing women's needs
1. What needs and opportunities exist for increasing women's productivity and/or production?
2. What needs and opportunities exist for increasing women's access to and control of resources?
3. What needs and opportunities exist for increasing women's access to and control of benefits?
4. How do these needs and opportunities relate to the country's other general and sectoral development needs and opportunities?
5. Have women been directly consulted in identifying such needs and opportunities?

Defining general project objectives
1. Are project objectives explicitly related to women's needs?
2. Do these objectives adequately reflect women's needs?
3. Have women participated in setting those objectives?
4. Have there been any earlier efforts?
5. How has the present proposal built on earlier activity?

Identifying possible negative effects
1. Might the project reduce women's access to or control of resources and benefits?
2. Might it adversely affect women's situation in some other way?
3. What will be the effects on women in the short and longer term?

WOMEN'S DIMENSION IN PROJECT DESIGN
Project impact on women's activities
1. Which of these activities (production, reproduction and maintenance, socio-political) does the project affect?
2. Is the planned component consistent with the current gender denomination for the activity?
3. If it is planned to change the women's performance of that activity, ie. locus of activity, remunerative mode, technology, mode of activity) is this feasible,, and what positive or negative effects would there be on women?

continued...

Example of Harvard Tool 4: Checklist

4. If it does not change it, is this a missed opportunity for women's roles in the development process?
5. How can the project design be adjusted to increase the above-mentioned positive effects, and reduce or eliminate the negative ones?

Project impact on women's access and control

1. How will each of the project components affect women's access to and control of the resources and benefits engaged in and stemming from the production of goods and services?
2. How will each of the project components affect women's access to and control of the resources and benefits engaged in and stemming from the reproduction and maintenance of the human resources?
3. How will each of the project components affect women's access to and control of the resources and benefits engaged in and stemming from the socio-political functions?
4. What forces have been set into motion to induce further exploration of constraints and possible improvements?
5. How can the project design be adjusted to increase women's access to and control of resources and benefits?

WOMEN'S DIMENSION IN PROJECT IMPLEMENTATION
Personnel

1. Are project personnel aware of and sympathetic towards women's needs?
2. Are women used to deliver the goods or services to women beneficiaries?
3. Do personnel have the necessary skills to provide any special inputs required by women?
4. What training techniques will be used to develop delivery systems?
5. Are there appropriate opportunities for women to participate in project management positions?

Organisational structures

1. Does the organisational form enhance women's access to resources?
2. Does the organisation have adequate power to obtain resources needed by women from other organisations?
3. Does the organisation have the institutional capability to support and protect women during the change process?

Operations and logistics

1. Are the organisation's delivery channels accessible to women in terms of personnel, location and timing?
2. Do control procedures exist to ensure dependable delivery of the goods and services?
3. Are there mechanisms to ensure that the project resources or benefits are not usurped by males?

Finances

1. Do funding mechanisms exist to ensure programme continuity?
2. Are funding levels adequate for proposed tasks?
3. Is preferential access to resources by males avoided?

continued...

4. Is it possible to trace funds for women from allocation to delivery with a fair degree of accuracy?

Flexibility

1. Does the project have a management information system which will allow it to detect the effects of the operation on women?
2. Does the organisation have enough flexibility to adapt its structures and operations to meet the changing or new-found situations of women?

WOMEN'S DIMENSION IN PROJECT EVALUATION
Data requirements

1. Does the project's monitoring and evaluation system explicitly measure the project's effects on women?
2. Does it also collect data to update the Activity Analysis and the Women's Access and Control Analysis?
3. Are women involved in designating the data requirements?

Data collection and analysis

1. Are the data collected with sufficient frequency so that necessary project adjustments could be made during the project?
2. Are the data fed back to project personnel and beneficiaries in an understandable form and on a timely basis to allow project adjustments?
3. Are women involved in the collection and interpretation of data?
4. Are data analysed so as to provide guidance to the design of other projects?
5. Are key areas of WID/GAD research identified?

Source: Overholt, Anderson, Cloud and Austin, Gender Roles in Development Projects, Kumarian Press Inc, Connecticut, 1985

Case study of the Harvard Analytical Framework: Indonesia Community Forestry Project

This case study is adapted from *Two Halves Make a Whole: Balancing Gender Relations in Development,* published by CCIC, MATCH, AQOCI, Ottawa 1991, and reproduced in Oxfam's *Gender Training Manual.* Here, it is included as an illustration of the Harvard Analytical Framework, even though it seems that this framework was not actually used in planning the project. The case study is reproduced here in minimal detail. For planning purposes, more detail would be needed before the following data could be considered sufficient.

Project background

This community forestry project was approved in 1983, in the village of Biyasan (not its real name) in Indonesia. It was part of a programme developed by the Indonesian Ministry of Forestry in order to make forestry benefit local communities as well was state and business interests. Poverty in Biyasan was a result of the complex relationship between high population density, poor quality soil, inequitable land-tenure traditions, and out-migration of men. The poorest people tended to live in households headed by women – 20% of the total. In a further 10%, the male family heads had migrated in search of waged employment. Most families had lived in Biyasan for generations, but a number were resettled into the area and had been allocated 0.5 hectares of land. The nearby forests were becoming depleted because of widespread clear-cutting and selling of timber. The land-use profile gave the following picture.

38%   Agricultural production

12%   Home gardens

7%   Private woodlots

15%   Fallow

33%   Unproductive (Adapted from Match 1991, pp 122-4)

Using Harvard Tool 1: Activity Profile

As stated above, the first tool of the Harvard Analytical Framework helps to collate data about men's and women's activities. For the people in the project area, the gender division of labour could be represented as in the table overleaf. In addition to such a quick overview, it is important to examine the details of who does what. Which women carry out a task? Which men? Where? When? For how long? In this case study, important information could have been gleaned by asking questions on the following issues:

- Wealthy farmers employed agricultural wage labour (men and women) at harvest time as well as using family labour.

- Poorer farmers relied on unpaid family labour and assistants.

- Poor farmers could not rely only on their farms to sustain their families; they needed to earn income in other ways as well.

- Reforestry had provided employment for a number of men and women, but these jobs had decreased. Women had been the main wage labourers in tree nurseries. Many women worked as unpaid labourers alongside their husbands who were employed by the state forestry company.

- Women were active in local rotating credit and savings schemes.

- Girls were involved in household work from an early age. At age 7, they helped feed animals, carry water, and gather fuel wood. By the time they were 10 years old, girls were helping plant and harvest rice. There was a village school but many girls, especially those whose mothers worked as labourers or market traders, had to drop out.

- Boys were active in feeding and caring for the animals and helping with their father's work. (Adapted from Match 1991, pp 122, 124, 129).

Using Harvard Tool 1: Activity profile

Production activities	Male Child	Male Adult	Woman Child	Woman Adult
Planting, weeding, storing rice			x	x
Harvesting rice			x	x
Seedling production		x		x
Cassava cultivation		x		
Maize cultivation		x		
Tobacco growing		x		x
Peanut cultivation		x		x
Cashew cultivation		x		
Coffee growing		x		x
Cocoa growing		x		
Home gardens				x
Seasonal agricultural work		x		x
Contract labourers		x		
Reforestation		x		x
Production, sale of rattan items				x
Crafts and sales		x		
Nursery reforestation				x
Animal breeding		x		
Transplanting				x
Hoeing				x
Weeding				x
Harvesting				x
Picking and drying coffee				x
Picking and drying tobacco				x
Gathering leaves and fruit				x
Ploughing fields		x		
Terrace construction		x		
Reproduction activities				
Household work			x	x
Feeding cattle	x		x	x
Collecting firewood	x		x	x
Collecting water			x	x
Collecting natural medicines			x	x
Animal care	x			
Socio-political activities[6]				
Weddings		x		x
Funerals		x		x
Participation in arisan				x
Village meetings		x		x

Source: Match 1991, p 129

Using Harvard Tool 2: Access and Control Profile

The Indonesian forestry project used Tool 2 (for examining men and women's access to and control over resources and benefits) to collect data which is partially represented in the table below. This tool indicates who has access to resources and control over their use. Benefits realised from household (and community) production and use of resources are also identified and listed. Columns indicate whether or not women and men have access to them, and control over their use.

However, use of Harvard Tool 2 reveals more data than can be shown in the table. It is necessary to examine which men and which women have access or control, and to ask what is actually meant by access and control for each case.

Such questions for this project would reveal the following details.

- Women and men both owned and inherited land, although women only owned 32% of all productive land. Very few farmers were landless sharecroppers. The average size of holding was 0.7 hectares, with 6% of the population holding more than 3.5 hectares.

- Wealthier farmers could obtain credit, and some had access to machinery for weeding and hulling.

- Women's earnings traditionally came from making rattan products and other non-wood forest goods and trading in the market.

- Wage labour had dropped significantly over recent years. It now accounted for 30% of male income and 17% of female income. There were few employment opportunities for women.

- Women traditionally did not benefit as much as men from credit and extension programmes for farmers. (Adapted from Match 1991, 121).

Using Harvard Tool 2: Access and control profile					
Resources			Benefits		
	Women	Men		Women	Men
Land	A/C	A/C	Credit programme		A/C
Credit		A/C	Extension programme	A	A/C
Machines		A/C	Planting and work in nursery	A	A/C
Fertilizer		A/C	Stoves provided by project	A	A/C
Paid work	A/C	A/C	Incentives		A/C
Key: A = Access, C = Control					

Source: Match 1991, p 130

Using Harvard Tool 3: Influencing Factors

If the Harvard Analytical Framework had been used in the project at the outset, as a planning tool, planners would have taken into account the influencing factors which shape gender relations and provide different opportunities and constraints for women and men. For instance, these factors would have included the different impact of changing migration patterns on women and men, and which women or men were most affected.

Tool 3 can also be used to examine, in retrospect, some of the key changes in gender relations that arose from the case-studies project activities.

Economic: Paid work in the project was more often given to men.

Social: Implementation of the project changed the socio-economic relations between men and women to the further advantage of men. Men gained power, women lost some.

Environment: Women were replaced by men in seedling production in the nursery. Environmental management is mostly the responsibility of upper-class men.

Education: Women did not have access to training activities, credit, and extension services. They were also excluded from training and marketing of ovens. (Match 1991, p 130)

Using Harvard Tool 4: Checklist

The checklist creates a wealth of data for any project. For reasons of space, we have chosen not to illustrate the checklist for this case study. If the Harvard Analytical Framework had been used for planning, the checklist would have highlighted in advance many of the problems which arose subsequently.

People-Oriented Planning Framework

Background

The Framework for People-Oriented Planning in Refugee Situations (popularly called POP) is an adaptation of the Harvard Analytical Framework. It was adapted for use in refugee situations, but also in order to overcome some of the Harvard Framework's initial weaknesses. POP was devised for the United Nations High Commission on Refugees (UNHCR), by Mary B Anderson and the UNHCR Senior Coordinator for Refugee Women, M (Brazeau) Howarth, following the adoption by UNHCR of a Policy on Refugee Women. It was developed with funding from the Canadian International Development Agency (CIDA).

The information included here is adapted from Anderson, Brazeau and Overholt, *A Framework for People-Oriented Planning in Refugee Situations Taking Account of Women*, published by UNHCR, Geneva, 1992.

Aims of the Framework

The central purpose of POP is to ensure that there is an efficient and equitable distribution of resources and services. The framework aims to promote more appropriate targeting of development assistance, and more efficient use of donors' resources. It also aims to 'ensure [that] disparities between the sexes are reduced' (Anderson 1992, 1).

The Framework

In the introduction to the POP framework, the following key factors are emphasised:

Change: When people flee from disaster or conflict, their lives change rapidly and dramatically, and continue to change. Even in long-term refugee settlements where women's and men's roles may stabilise, these will be different from those which existed before the flight, and the new roles may be regarded as temporary by refugees themselves. In some situations, there will be a stronger adherence to traditional roles, values and perceptions. Conversely, a crisis may open up avenues for change which can lead to more balanced relations between men and women. The dynamics of change working within the society determine, to a great extent, the acceptance and success of any project.

Participation: Refugee participation is a major factor in determining whether or not a project will succeed. This requires the involvement of refugee women, men, and children.

Importance of analysis: Whatever type of project is being planned (water, food distribution, health promotion, and so on), socio-economic and demographic analysis are critical components of project planning.

Components of the Framework

The POP Framework has three components:

- The Determinants Analysis, (also called the Refugee Population Profile and Context Analysis);

- The Activities Analysis;

- The Use and Control of Resources Analysis.

POP Tool 1: Refugee Population Profile and Context Analysis

Two aspects shape the roles and responsibilities of men and women in refugee situations. The first is the population profile both of the displaced groups and of their host community or country. Second, the social and cultural context of both refugees and hosts will influence, possibly change, the gender division of use and control of resources. The following questions can serve as a guide in drawing up a populations profile and gaining an insight into the contexts.

Who are the refugees?
Answering this question involves assessing the refugee population from a demographic perspective. Who are the refugees? For example, are they families or individuals? Women? Men? Children? Are the children accompanied or not? This kind of assessment must take place at the earliest stage of a refugee emergency – details can be gathered at a later stage. It is important to find out the composition of the refugee group before they became refugees, and subsequent changes in that composition.

What is the refugees' context?
Factors which will have shaped gender relations before the flight and during asylum are broad and interrelated, but may include the following.

- Community norms and social hierarchy, such as family/ community power structures and religious beliefs, can be particularly important among refugee groups where men's and women's roles are changing;

- Demographic factors;

- Institutional structures, including the nature of government bureaucracies, and arrangements for the generation and dissemination of knowledge, technology, and skills;

- General economic conditions, such as poverty levels, inflation rates, income distribution, international terms of trade, and infrastructure;

- Internal and external political events;

- Legal parameters;

- Training and education;

- The attitudes of the host country/ community;

- The attitude of refugees to development/ assistance workers (Anderson 1992, pp 4-5).

As stated above, similar questions should be asked for the host and the refugee population.

The purpose of identifying these determinants is to consider which ones affect activities or resources, and how they are affected by them. This helps you identify external constraints and opportunities which you must consider in planning your programmes in order to better predict your inputs.

POP Tool 2: The Activities Analysis

Similar to the Harvard Tool 1 (Activities Profile), this tool enables you to find out who does what, as well as when and where they do it. Because the gender division of labour and roles is disrupted by flight, it is essential to find out what women and men were doing before, and what they are doing now, or are able to do, in the refugee situation. How strictly defined was, and is, the division of labour? Do adults or children carry out a particular task now? Was this different before? Which tasks used to be done every seasonal, which ones were carried out every day, and is this the same now? How long do the tasks take? Where are they carried out? How does this differ from before?

The activities analysis must be linked to the population profile, for a very good reason: if refugees are mainly men, then the jobs which women normally undertook cannot be done in the usual way.

Protection is a crucial concern, particularly for women and girls. The activity of protecting – including who offers protection under which circumstances – is both a legal and social concern: refugees have often lost their national status, as well as the social networks which may have offered them some protection. Communities provide protection through a protection hierarchy. This may involve communities (families and other social groupings) protecting individuals; men protecting women; adults protecting children. Such protection can be of a legal, physical or social nature. It is important to find out what protection gaps there are in the current situation. For example, what mechanisms are there for protecting orphaned children? (Anderson 1992, p 5)

POP Tool 2: Activities Analysis

The table below illustrates the Activities Analysis. This analysis should be completed for both the pre-refugee situation and the current situation.

Example of POP Tool 2: Activities analysis				
Activities	Who?	Where?	When? /How long?	Resources used

Production of goods...
eg carpentry
    metal work
... and services
eg teaching
    domestic labour				

Agriculture
eg land clearance
    planting
    care of livestock				

Household production
eg childcare
    home garden
    water collection				

Protection activities
eg of unaccompanied
    children
    single women
    elderly people				

Social, political, religious activities eg community meeting ceremonies				

Adapted from Anderson 1992, p 8

POP Tool 3: Use and Control of Resources Analysis

Similar to the Harvard Tool 2 (Access and Control Profile), this tool helps you determine how resources are distributed, and who has a say over their use, by asking the following questions.

- What resources do people have/ which did they bring with them?

- Who has which resources?

- What resources must be provided for which refugees?

You can identify what resources were used and controlled by women and men before flight, and what resources they now control and use as refugees.

This includes both material resources and intangible ones, such as community structures, social networks, time, labour, and education. Women and men may have lost some resources (such as land, full-time employment, or membership of a social network) and may be unable to regain them.

Men, women, and children will have lost different resources. They may also have gained new ones, for example, access to food items distributed by aid agencies. The new situation will affect gender relations, and may introduce opportunities for positive change for women.

Example of POP Tool 3: Use of resources analysis

Resource lost due to flight	Who used this (gender/age)	Who controlled this (gender/age)
land livestock shelter tools education system health care income		
Resource brought by refugees	Who has this (gender/age)	Who uses this (gender/age)

Skills
eg political
   manufacturing
   carpentry
   sewing
   cleaning
   agricultural
   animal husbandry
 	
Knowledge
eg literacy
   teaching
   medicine/health		

Resource provided to refugees	To whom is this provided (gender/age)	How/where/when is it provided (through males? females? adults?)
food shelter clothing education legal services health-care services etc.		

Source: Anderson 1992, p 11

Commentary

Joint Commentary on Harvard Framework and POP

(These points are relevant to both the frameworks. They should be read in conjunction with the individual commentaries on each framework which follow, where points relevant specifically to each framework are addressed.)

Uses

For data collection and analysis

The gender frameworks are useful in gathering and analysing information. This analysis can then provide a database for any stage of a project cycle. The gender frameworks are more appropriate for projects than for programmes, because they rely on micro-level analysis. You need detailed knowledge of the social groups in question, so it is difficult to use them to study a region where people's social and economic circumstances differ widely.

In training

They are often used in training programmes to illustrate to emergency workers and planners the complexity of a refugee situation.

As a gender-neutral 'entry point'

These gender frameworks can be useful for starting a discussion about gender issues with counterparts who are resistant to thinking about power dynamics between women and men, because they are clearly based on fact, not theory.

For communication

The gender frameworks rely on the economic argument of most efficient allocation of resources. It therefore uses language similar to that of economists, which can be particularly useful when talking to people whose main influence is mainstream economic thought.

In conjunction with the Moser Framework

The gender frameworks are frequently used in conjunction with the Moser Framework, which enables planners to include Moser's concept of strategic gender interests.

Why they appeal

Practical and hands-on

Give a clear picture of the gender division of labour

When the data have been collected, the gender frameworks give a clear and simple picture of who does what, when, and what with. They make women's work visible and help you avoid making serious technical blunders such as handing out resources at inappropriate times, or underestimating women's existing workload. They can clearly show differences in workloads, and in access to and control of resources.

Distinguish between access and control of resources

Easily adaptable

Non-threatening and gender-neutral; they rely on facts rather than theory

Potential limitations and adaptations

Developed from an efficiency perspective, rather than an equity perspective

Both gender frameworks were developed from the WID efficiency approach, so they suffer from similar theoretical constraints. They were designed not so much to create more balanced gender relations, but to allocate new resources in such a way as to increase the efficiency of the project or programme. The gender frameworks therefore give no guidance on how development workers might challenge existing inequalities. Neither do they draw out power dynamics, show the relationships between different people, or how people bargain, negotiate interests, make decisions, and so on. Thus, using Kabeer's definitions of gender-aware policies (see p 21), the gender frameworks will tend to lead to gender-neutral or gender-specific interventions rather than to ones which transform gender relations.

For instance, in parts of the world where women have a very reduced role in production, the logic of the gender frameworks would probably encourage development workers to work only with the men (who already have control). While this may be effective in raising the overall income of the household as a unit, the benefits do not necessarily reach the women, and the intervention will probably have tipped the balance of power further in favour of the men.

On the other hand, the gender frameworks can give the impression that giving any additional resources to women is a good thing. This is not necessarily the case. There are numerous examples of badly designed income-generation projects. In these cases, despite the fact that resources were given to women, the projects have ended up further disadvantaging women. They have become time-consuming burdens for women or made a loss, not a profit.

Encourage an insufficiently thorough analysis

The matrices can encourage people to take a fairly superficial, tick-the-boxes approach to data collection. Planners can end up feeling over-confident, assuming that they know all they need to know. They can thereby miss the complexities of the community's reality, and can miss crucial opportunities for change.

Fail to specify the importance of the participation of women and men themselves in the analysis

The matrices do not specifically require that planners ensure that the community members themselves – women as well as men – analyse their situation. If the Harvard or POP gender frameworks are the only planning tools used, they will lead to very top-down plans.

Some people have successfully used the matrices participatively, i.e. filling in the matrices with members of the community and discussing the results with them. They have found it effective in raising gender issues. Other users report that they have found it difficult to use with communities. One criticism in particular is that the distinction between access and control has been difficult to convey.

Do not address the culture and context of the institutions which determine the allocation of resources to recipients

Both the Harvard and the POP gender frameworks assume that institutions, including development organisations, have a neutral culture regarding gender power relations. Increasingly, it is understood that the way in which an organisation is 'gendered' (see pp 9-15) has a large impact on how successful their planning is in terms of supporting fairer gender relations and/ or women's empowerment.

Emphasise separation rather than connectedness and inter-relationships between individuals and groups

The Harvard and POP Gender frameworks concentrate on the activities and resources of different categories of people, rather than on relationships between different groups. This leads to an emphasis on men and women, old and young, as separate groups with different and separate activities. However, the inter-relationships between them, and the forms of household and community co-operation and exchange are not examined. For instance, in exchange for his wife's labour on his fields, a husband may be obliged to pay her wages or to work on her fields in return. The exchange may be less direct. In return for giving a male relation control over a loan which is in her name, a woman may increase her status, or be more secure in times of the hunger gap.

Decision-making processes may be much more complicated than those represented in either matrix. Looking only at production cycles, and access and control over resources does not give a full picture of the negotiations and decision-making processes over key stages; the result is an incomplete picture of relationships. Consider a case where producers sell their wares to an intermediary, who gives them a very low price for the goods. It may seem obvious to an NGO to take over and replace the intermediary, and offer a better price. However, it may also be the case that the intermediary offers the producers informal patronage and support in times of hardship, such as credit or employment opportunities. This connection would not be visible in the Harvard framework but any attempt in these circumstances to replace the intermediary without considering this patronage is likely to fail.

In addition, control over a resource may only be partial. You may assume that a woman has control over purchase of seeds. In fact, the state marketing structures and the intermediaries also have a high level of control, because they can dictate what is available, and at what price.

Issues of power are not made explicit

Neither the Harvard nor the POP Gender frameworks ask how and why gender relations are unequal; and so issues of power distribution are not drawn out. Because the way in which men and women relate to each other is not examined, the underlying causes of women's subordination are often not tackled. However, the profiles which emerge of women's and men's roles can be entry points for examining these issues, for example comparing differences in the access and control of resources.

Adaptation: Consultants for the Netherlands Development Assistance (NEDA) at the Ministry of Foreign Affairs adapted the Harvard and POP frameworks in 1994 to address this issue. Their framework is published in the manual *Gender Assessment Studies*. In it, a third profile, of women's socio-political position, is added to both gender frameworks, as in the matrix below.

Adaptation of Harvard Tool 2: Women's socio-political profile			
Women's socio-political position compared to men's	Lower (worse)	About Equal	Higher (better)
1. Women's participation in decision-making: • in the household • at community level • society at large			
2. (Self) image: Self image of women Image of women in society			
3. Organisational capacity			
4. Other			

Source: quoted in Monitoring and Evaluation from a Gender Perspective: A Guideline, SNV, March 1995

Ignore other underlying inequalities

As originally designed, neither the Harvard Framework nor the POP Framework deals with other underlying inequalities such as class or race; nor do they consider the different types of household in various contexts. Users are asked to compare 'women' and 'men' as two separate, homogeneous groups. Even within a particular cultural group, the differences between mothers-in-law and daughters-in-law, or first wife and second wife, or compound head and unmarried son, may be very marked. At worst, this over-simplification means that users may ignore the complex power differentials which exist in the real world, and fail to determine who the most vulnerable people are.

Adaptation: It is possible to adapt the Harvard and POP frameworks to take account of underlying inequalities. Data would be disaggregated according to cultural, ethnic, and economic factors as well as gender and age. Alternatively, different matrices can filled in for each relatively homogeneous group

Designed for information collection, not for planning
The Harvard and POP gender frameworks see the need for better information as the central issue for gender analysis. As a consequence, they provide no guidance for planners as to what action should logically follow this collection of information.

(Below, additional users' points on the two gender frameworks are listed separately.)

Additional commentary on the Harvard Framework only

Potential limitations and adaptations
Too materialistic
By concentrating on activities and material resources rather than relationships between people, the Harvard Framework takes tangible considerations as its starting point for analysis. It tends to assume that people make rational choices based purely on material considerations, thus leaving out some crucial motivational factors and constraints, such as community dynamics and cultural values. To counter this tendency, you can adapt the framework by adding intangible resources to the Access and Control Profile, bringing in variables such as membership of networks or kinship groups.

Oversimplifies the concepts of access and control
The Harvard Framework can encourage a simplistic 'yes or no' approach by asking whether or not women have access and control. However, women experience a much more complex reality. For example, a women's group may have access to some village land, and have partial control in that they can decide what crops to grow and how. But it may be up to the elders to decide which plot the women are given. Looking simply at access and control can also hide the bargaining processes which take place in order to arrive at such complicated outcomes.

Changes over time are not taken into account
The matrices of the Harvard Framework tend to give a static view of the community. However, an awareness of changes over time in gender relations can be crucial for spotting opportunities as well as areas where pressures are increasing or might soon arise.

Adaptations: In one possible adaptation which addresses this issue, the person compiling the matrix questions at each stage whether a certain state of affairs has changed, and why. In another adaptation, the data for the matrix is gathered twice, as it is for the POP framework: once to look at the current situation, and once to compare it to an appropriate point in the past.

Does not place emphasis on who performs community work
The framework prioritises productive and reproductive activities. It does not encourage you to think about tasks that are undertaken for community cohesion (discussed in Moser's 'triple roles' concept, pp 56-57).

Adaptation: Instead of including only the categories of productive and reproductive activities, a third category is often added – either social, political, religious, or 'community activities'.

Additional commentary on POP Framework only

Uses

In planning for refugee situations
POP is a practical tool to assist in planning in refugee situations. With a little adaptation, it is also useful in emergencies or during periods of rapid change.

Why it appeals

Specifically designed for use in refugee situations

Simple, step-by-step approach
The framework is conceptually simple, and easy to administer. It is therefore suited to the exigencies of emergency work, even in the initial stages when workers do not have the time to employ more complex techniques. The framework pulls together a very rich map of refugee profile and socio-economic data and does so more rapidly than, for example, some forms of participative or rapid rural appraisal (PRA, RRA).

Includes concepts of change over time and protection
Two elements of the POP Framework are particularly significant for gender relations in refugee groups. The first is the element of change over time, which enables planners to consider the long term as well as the short term. The second element is the need of vulnerable groups for protection, and the fact that such protection should be considered as an activity which someone has to provide.

Uses an expanded concept of resources
The POP Framework expands the concept of resources used in the Harvard Framework, progressing beyond consideration only of material resources, to include less tangible things such as skills and social organisation, and – very important for women – time. It highlights the importance of resources in relation to responsibilities. It brings out the idea that communities lose some resources over time, but also retain some and gain others. The POP framework can help to find indicators which reveal whether the gap between women and men in terms of benefits is widening or narrowing.

Potential limitations

Works best with homogeneous groups
It is difficult to use across a region or group of communities which may not be totally homogeneous. In a refugee camp with very different communities, one needs to apply the framework first to each group independently.

Question of control cannot be fully answered
The question of who has control in the community cannot be fully answered when control over most aspects of social life is assumed by external actors.

Short-term interventions may be the result
Not enough emphasis is given to the long-term development of refugee or displaced communities.

Further reading

The Harvard Analytical Framework is presented in Overholt, Anderson, Austin, and Cloud (1985) *Gender Roles in Development Projects*, published by Kumarian Press Inc, Connecticut; a second edition has been published by Lynne Rienner Publishers.

The POP Framework is explained in a well-presented and easy-to-read 14-page guide in Overholt C A, Anderson M, (Brazeau) Howarth *A Framework for People-Oriented Planning in Refugee Situations Taking Account of Women, Men and Children: A Practical Planning Tool for Refugee Workers*, United Nations High Commission for Refugees, Geneva, 1992.

In addition, another handbook of 45 pages gives a sector-by-sector guide to using the framework (for example, for water provision, or for food distribution). This book includes the lessons learned by the UNHCR in sectoral programming. Anderson M, *A UNHCR Handbook. People-Oriented Planning At Work: Using POP to Improve UNHCR Programming*, Collaborative for Development Action Inc, Geneva, 1994.

Consultants working for the Netherlands Development Assistance (NEDA) at the Ministry of Foreign Affairs, The Hague, Netherlands, adapted the Harvard and POP frameworks. Their work is published by the Institute of Social Studies Advisory Service: Lingen A with Brouwers R, Nugieren M, Plantenga D, and Zuidberg L (1997) *Gender Assessment Studies: A Manual for Gender Consultants.*

2.3 | Moser Framework

Background

In reaction to the Women in Development (WID) approach, which in the 1970s encouraged treating women's issues as separate concerns, the Gender and Development (GAD) approach argued for an integrated gender-planning perspective in all development work, concentrating on the power relations between women and men. This approach challenges many of the assumptions behind traditional planning methods.

The Moser Framework was part of this challenge. Caroline Moser developed it as a method of gender analysis at the Development Planning Unit (DPU), University of London, UK in the early 1980s. Moving from analysis into action, Caroline Moser, with Caren Levy of the DPU, further developed it into a gender policy and planning method. Moser's method was presented as a mainstream planning methodology in its own right, like urban or transport planning. The following section is adapted from Moser's book *Gender Planning and Development: Theory, Practice and Training*, Routledge, London, 1993. It also draws on a discussion of Moser's framework by the Canadian Council for International Co-operation in *Two Halves Make a Whole: Balancing Gender Relations in Development*, MATCH, Ottawa, 1991.

Since Moser left the DPU in 1986, their Gender Policy and Planning Programme has produced a methodology which has evolved to meet the need for strategies to integrate gender in all types of intervention, and to confront power relations in organisations, communities, and social institutions. It has been used by a wide range of development organisations. Since it has not been used by Oxfam to date, and we can therefore not provide a users' commentary, the DPU methodology is included as an appendix (p 123).

Aims of the framework

As stated above, the Moser Framework aims to set up 'gender planning' as a type of planning in its own right: 'The goal of gender planning is the emancipation of women from their subordination, and their achievement of equality, equity, and empowerment. This will vary widely in different contexts, depending on the extent to which women as a category are subordinated in status to men as a category.' (Moser 1993, 1)

The Moser Framework questions assumptions that planning is a purely technical task. Moser characterises gender planning as distinct from traditional planning methods in several critical ways: 'First, [gender planning] is both political and technical in nature. Second, it assumes conflict in the planning process. Third, it involves transformatory processes. Fourth, it characterises planning as "debate".' (Moser 1993, 87)

The Framework

At the heart of the Moser Framework are three concepts:

- Women's triple role;

- Practical and strategic gender needs;

- Categories of WID/GAD policy approaches (policy matrix).

Moser Tool 1: Gender roles identification / triple role

This tool involves mapping the gender division of labour by asking 'who does what?' Caroline Moser identifies a 'triple role' for low-income women in most societies, which she uses in this framework. The triple role for women consists of reproductive, productive, and community-managing activities. In contrast, men primarily undertake productive and community politics activities.

Reproductive work: As defined by Moser, this involves the care and maintenance of the household and its members, including bearing and caring for children, preparing food, collecting water and fuel, shopping, housekeeping, and family health-care. In poor communities, reproductive work is, for the most part, labour-intensive and time-consuming. It is almost always the responsibility of women and girls.

Productive work: This involves the production of goods and services for consumption and trade (in employment and self-employment). Both women and men can be involved in productive activities, but their functions and responsibilities often differ. Women's productive work is often less visible and less valued than men's.

Community work: These activities include the collective organisation of social events and services – ceremonies and celebrations, activities to improve the community, participation in groups and organisations, local political activities, and so on. This type of work is seldom considered in economic analyses, yet it involves considerable volunteer time and is important for the spiritual and cultural development of communities. It is also a vehicle for community organisation and self-determination. Both women and men engage in community activities, although a gender division of labour also prevails here. (MATCH 1991, 26) Moser divides community work into two different types of work.

Community-managing activities are undertaken primarily by women as an extension of their reproductive role. Such activities ensure the provision and maintenance of scarce resources which everyone uses, such as water, health-care, and education. This is voluntary unpaid work, carried out during women's 'free' time.

Community politics are undertaken primarily by men, who take part in organised, formal politics, often within the framework of national politics. They are usually paid in cash for this work, or benefit indirectly through improved status or power. (MATCH 1991, 34)

Women, men, boys, and girls are all likely to take some part in each of these areas of work, but men are much less likely to be involved in reproductive work. In many societies, women and girls do almost all of the reproductive as well as much of the productive work. As the Moser framework recognises that women perform reproductive and community-management activities along-side productive work, it makes visible work that tends to be invisible. Ultimately, it aims to ensure that tasks are equally valued. Reproductive work is crucial to human survival, and to the maintenance and reproduction of the labour force, yet it is seldom considered 'real' work. For instance, when people are asked what work they do, their responses are usually related to productive work, especially paid or income-generating work.

It makes sense to use the triple-role analysis in a planning framework, because any development intervention in one area of work will affect the activities performed in the other two areas. For example, women's repro-ductive workload can prevent them from participating in development projects. When they do participate, the additional time spent farming, producing goods, attending training sessions or meetings, means less time spent on other tasks such as child-care or food preparation.

Moser Tool 2: Gender needs assessment

The Moser Framework's second tool builds on Maxine Molyneux's (1985) concept of women's gender interests. Moser's concept is based on the idea that women as a group have particular needs, which differ from those of men as a group; not only because of women's triple work role, but also because of their subordinate position to men in most societies. Similar to Molyneux's concepts of practical and strategic gender interests, Moser distinguishes between two types of gender needs.

Practical gender needs: Moser defines practical gender needs as those which, if they were met, would assist women in their current activities. Interventions which focus on meeting practical gender needs respond to an immediate perceived necessity in a specific context, often related to inadequacies in living conditions. Meeting practical gender needs does not challenge the existing gender division of labour or women's subordinate position in society, although these are the causes of women's practical gender needs. (MATCH 1991, 40)

Development interventions which are intended to meet women's practical gender needs may include:

- Water provision;

- Health-care provision;

- Opportunities for earning an income to provide for the household;

- Provision of housing and basic services;

- Distribution of food.

These needs are shared by all household members, yet women often identify them as their specific needs, because it is women who assume responsibility for meeting their families' requirements.

Strategic gender needs: Moser defines these as the needs which, if they were met, would enable women to transform existing imbalances of power between women and men. Women's strategic gender needs are those which exist because of women's subordinate social status. Strategic gender needs vary in particular contexts. They relate to gender divisions of labour, power, and control, and may include such issues as legal rights, domestic violence, equal wages, and women's control over their own bodies. Meeting strategic gender needs helps women to achieve greater equality and challenges their subordinate position, including their role in society. (MATCH 1991, 39)

Interventions which address women's strategic gender needs may include:

- Challenges to the gender division of labour;

- Alleviation of the burden of domestic labour and child care;

- The removal of institutionalised forms of discrimination such as laws and legal systems biased in favour of men;

- Provision of reproductive health services, offering women choice over child-bearing

- Measures against male violence. (Molyneux 1985)

Moser Tool 3: Disaggregating control of resources and decision-making within the household

This tool asks the questions: Who controls what? Who decides what? How?

Here the Moser Framework links allocation of resources within the household (intra-household allocation) with the bargaining processes which determine this. Who has control over what resources within the household, and who has what power of decision-making?

Moser Tool 4: Planning for balancing the triple role

Users of the framework are asked to examine whether a planned programme or a project will increase a woman's workload in one of her roles, to the detriment of her other roles. Women must balance competing demands on their reproductive, productive, and community responsibilities. The need to balance these roles determines women's involvement in each of the roles, and potentially constrains their involvement in activities which will significantly increase the time they need to spend in one particular role.

Moser also highlights how sectoral planning (which concentrates only on one area, such as transport, and is commonly undertaken by governments) has very often been particularly detrimental to women, since it does not consider the interplay between women's triple roles. Carrying out intersectoral, or linked, planning would avoid this problem.

Moser Tool 5: Distinguishing between different aims in interventions: the WID/GAD Policy Matrix

This is mainly a tool for evaluation, to examine what approach has been used in an existing project, programme, or policy. However, it can also be used to consider what would be most suitable approach for future work. Examining the policy approaches can help you anticipate some of their inherent weaknesses, constraints, and possible pitfalls.

The Moser Framework encourages users to consider how different planning interventions transform the subordinate position of women, by asking: to what extent do different approaches meet practical and/ or strategic gender needs? To support this, Moser gives an analysis of five different types of policy approach which have dominated development planning over the last few decades, which she defines as the welfare, equity, anti-poverty, efficiency, and empowerment approach. These different policy approaches have not occurred in strict chronological order. In practice, many have appeared more or less simultaneously.

Welfare: This approach has existed since the 1950s. It was used most from 1950-70, but remains popular today. The welfare approach acknowledges women in their reproductive role only, and sees them as passive beneficiaries of development interventions. It aims to meet women's practical gender needs in their role as mothers, for example by providing food aid, implementing measures against malnutrition, and promoting family planning. The welfare approach can be characterised as 'top-down', and does not challenge the existing sexual division of labour or women's subordinate status.

Equity: This original WID approach was widely used in development work during the UN Women's Decade from 1976-85. Its purpose is to promote equality for women. The equity approach recognises women as active participants in development. It recognises the triple role, and seeks to meet women's strategic gender needs through direct state intervention, by giving women political and economic autonomy, and by reducing their inequality with men. The equity approach is criticised by some as rooted in Western notions of feminism, is often considered to be threatening to men, and is unpopular with most governments.

Anti-poverty: This is a less radical adaptation of the WID equity approach, adopted from the 1970s onwards. Using the argument that women are disproportionately represented among the poorest people, the purpose of the anti-poverty approach is to ensure that poor women move out of poverty by increasing their productivity. Thus, women's poverty is seen as a problem of underdevelopment, not of subordination. This approach recognises the productive role of women, and seeks to meet their practical gender need of earning an income, particularly in small-scale, income-generating projects. It is most popular with NGOs.

Efficiency: The third, and now predominant, adaptation of the WID approach has been adopted especially since debt crisis in the 1980s. Its purpose is to ensure that development is more efficient and effective through harnessing women's economic contribution. It seeks to meet women's practical gender needs, recognising all three roles. However, the efficiency approach often assumes that women's time is elastic, and women are expected to compensate for declining social services by simply extending their working day. It often wrongly associates women's 'participation' with increased gender equity and decision-making power for women. Despite these problems, it is still a very popular approach.

Empowerment: This is the most recent approach, articulated by Southern women. Its purpose is to empower women through supporting their own initiatives, thus fostering self-reliance. Women's subordination is seen not only as a result of male oppression, but also as a consequence of colonial and neo-colonial oppression.

The empowerment approach also recognises that women's experience is very varied, tempered by other factors such as class, race, age, and so on. It argues that action is necessary at different levels to combat the various aspects of women's oppression. The empowerment approach openly acknowledges the centrality of power – asserting that women have to get more of it in order to change their position. It recognises the triple role and seeks to meet strategic gender needs indirectly, through grassroots mobilisation of women, for example through organising women's groups which can make demands for their practical gender needs to be met (Moser 1993, 231).

Moser Tool 6: Involving women, and gender-aware organisations and planners, in planning

Finally, Moser's framework asks users to think about the importance of involving women, gender-aware organisations, and planners themselves in planning. This is essential to ensure that real practical and strategic gender needs are identified and incorporated into the planning process. These individuals or organisations must be involved not only in the analysis, but also in defining the goals of an intervention, and in its implementation.

Case study using Moser Framework

This case study refers to the Indonesia Forestry Project (pp 38-39) which has already been used as the case study for the Harvard Analytical Framework. The same case study is used here because some of the tools of the Moser Framework are similar to those of the Harvard Analytical Framework. Where this is the case, please refer to chapter 2.2 for full details, tables, and so on. Where a tool is unique to the Moser Framework, the full way of using it is shown here.

Using Moser Tool 1: Identifying gender roles/ triple role

This involves mapping who does what in a given community; the mapping is done in a similar way to the Activities Profile in the Harvard Analytical Framework (see p 33). When you use the Moser Framework, however, the roles and activities are analysed according to Moser's three categories of productive, reproductive, and community work.

Using Moser Tool 2: Gender needs assessment

This involves identifying women's practical and strategic gender needs – those needs they have as a consequence of their roles, tasks, and responsibilities; and those needs which, if they were met, would better enable them to challenge their existing inequality vis-à-vis men in their community.

For the Indonesia Forestry Project, the women's gender needs which were identified are listed in the table below.

Example of Moser Tool 2: Gender needs assessment	
Women's practical gender needs	Women's strategic gender needs
• access to seedlings • firewood • needs related to reforestation and forestry activities • improved ovens • marketing of rattan products • specific training • paid work	• collective organisation • right to speak out • skills in leadership, and leadership positions in the project and community • education

Adapted from MATCH 1991, 132

No attempt was made in the Indonesia project to address any of the poor women's strategic gender interests. In addition, women's practical needs related to forest management and forest products were not addressed.

Using Moser Tool 3: Disaggregating control of resources and decision-making within the household

For this case study, the data on who controls what, who decides what, and how, has already been presented in the Access and Control Profile in the Harvard Framework (p 34). However, not enough information was found out about which member of the household makes what decisions, and how. For good project planning, more detailed work would need to be done.

Using Moser Tool 4: Linked planning for balancing the triple role

This is about checking that all women's existing work and responsibilities have been fully considered and taken into account during planning. In this case, better project planning would have given more consideration to women's workload or how women balanced their triple role. This project concentrated almost exclusively on women's productive role. Consequently, planners made unrealistic assumptions about women's capacity to increase their productivity and participate in training activities.

Using Moser Tool 5: Analysing the policy aim, using the WID/GAD policy matrix

This tool examines the intervention's objectives, in the light of various WID/GAD approaches. In this case, the only project objective that mentions women states the aim to 'improve women's role in rural development and increase their productivity'. Therefore, the underlying policy approach was an anti-poverty one. Little consideration was given either of women's underlying subordination or of their non-productive roles.

If, on the other hand, the Indonesia Forestry Project had been designed using an empowerment approach, the planners would have sought out opportunities for women to discuss their practical needs in a way which would also begin to address some of the strategic needs. Supporting women's capacity to identify their own strategic needs and to find ways of addressing these would have become part of the project.

Using Moser Tool 6: Involving women, and gender-aware organisations and planners in planning

All the decision-makers in the Indonesia Forestry project were men. Women were able to exert some influence through the women's association. However, this did not include the community's poorer women, and only one woman was allowed to represent the association in the farmers' groups. The project would need to look at better ways to include poor women in the planning.

Commentary on Moser Framework

Uses

Planning at all levels

The Moser Framework can be used for planning at all levels, from regional to project planning. As shown in the case study above, elements of this framework are frequently used in conjunction with the Harvard Framework.

Training for awareness-raising, programme planning, and implementation

The Moser Framework is frequently used in training on gender issues to raise awareness of women's subordination, including their unequal workload, and to find potential ways of challenging these.

Why it appeals

Accessible and easily applicable

Many users find the Moser Framework easy to use. For instance, Sukey Field, a British gender trainer, reports that 'the Moser Framework is accessible, easily taught and communicated, and most groups from rural NGO to government workers find it easily applicable to their work'. Nazneen Kanji, of the London School of Economics, comments: 'An "adapted" Moser Framework is useful when dealing with high-level government and aid agency officials – [it is] less threatening than the Social Relations Approach [and] diffuses initial hostility'.

Moves 'planning' beyond technical concerns

The Moser Framework (and the literature on it) moves users from a purely technical approach to planning towards an understanding of its political significance. Planning is seen as transformatory, as likely to lead to conflict, and it is argued that it should be considered a 'debate'. The framework recognises that institutional/ political resistance to addressing, and transforming, gender relations is likely.

Speaks to planners in their own 'language'

Moser's Framework brings women's subordination into the planning discourse, and challenges planners in terms that they are familiar with.

Challenges inequality

Moser's concept of planning aims to challenge unequal gender relations and to support women's empowerment. The tools of the Moser Framework remind users that not all work carried out in the name of women in development does this.

Powerful tools of practical and strategic gender needs

The concepts of practical and strategic gender needs have proved powerful tools for judging the impact that a development intervention has on gender relations. In addition, the concepts remind development workers that women's short-term, practical needs must be addressed in a way which facilitates a more balanced relationship between men and women in the long term.

The concept of the triple role makes all areas of work visible
The triple role makes visible work that tends to be invisible, and helps to promote fairer valuing of tasks. It also reminds planners that productive, reproductive, and community work are interrelated. You cannot change one area without having an impact on the other sphere(s); and not all work takes place either in the household or in a designated workplace.

Distinguishes between policy approaches and thus encourages questioning an intervention's purpose
By categorising various WID/ GAD policy approaches to development, Moser helps you think through the main policy assumptions which are driving a particular project (and therefore alerts you to its possible shortcomings).

Potential limitations and adaptations

Radical agenda is depoliticised by the language of planning
The strength of speaking to planners of women's subordination in terms which they are familiar with has an accompanying weakness. To some extent, the nature of planning language depoliticises Moser's message. Although Moser's framework is based on an analysis of power and inequality, the chosen language does not fully capture the dynamics of gender power relations: the complex to and fro of bargaining, co-operation, and conflict. It is important to bear this loss of political forcefulness in mind, and to be ready to compensate for it as necessary.

In particular, talking of their gender 'needs' may make women and men appear passive – this is the language of top-down planning. In contrast, Molyneux's original use of 'interests' is related to concepts of rights and challenges to the structures of power. Talking about 'needs' can therefore inadvertently undermine Moser's attempts to address the issue of power disparity between planners and those targeted by planning. She attempts this in Tool 6, which requires users to consider how women should be involved directly in planning.

Concept of triple role does not fully capture the power imbalance between women and men
Although Moser uses the concept of gender 'roles' as a way to explore women's subordination, the word has many meanings in different contexts (for example, in sociology or in drama). In particular, the term can have a sense of a 'natural' or prescribed order of things; it can also imply that people have choice, as in 'my chosen role'. The concept of women's triple role is, therefore, weighted with other meanings of the word. These can result in side-stepping

the issue of how power relations are structured and played out. (Note that the concept of roles is not commonly used in other debates which address issues of structural inequality, such as racism or disability.)

Triple role or double role?
The triple role concept makes visible the time-consuming socio-political and cultural work which is essential to an understanding of social phenomena. But some people find it difficult to accept these three roles. Naila Kabeer (1995) argues that one weakness of the concept is that it does not strictly logically distinguish between 'who does what and how', and 'what is produced'.[7] The distinction between reproduction and production is clear: the former provides childcare and domestic work, the latter produces goods and services. But it is less clear whether community work refers to the production of a third type of resource, or to how the labour is organised (i.e. people working collectively rather than individually).

Kabeer argues that what is lost in this three-way distinction is the fact that most resources can be produced in a variety of settings, and through a variety of relationships. For example, if childcare is the resource, it can be produced through unpaid family labour, through collective unpaid labour in the form of crèches, through paid labour in the form of private day-care centres or domestic services. It can be provided by the family, by the community, the market, or the state. Each possibility will have very different consequences for the planning process and very different implications for women. Categorising such work as either reproductive or community-management work does not reveal all the opportunities for potential interventions, or foresee the possible impact of change on women's workload or status.

Women's and men's separate activities are emphasised, rather than relationships between the two
Like the Harvard and POP Frameworks, the Moser Framework emphasises what women and men do and the resources available to them, rather than focusing on the relationship between them, which determines how activities come to be performed by women or men, and the complex dynamics by which decisions are made. Even where the framework does examine issues of control or power, it still tends to over-emphasise the separation of women and men, rather than examining the ways in which women and men are connected.

Does not highlight other forms of inequality
Although Moser puts emphasis on the different types of households, and power differentials within households, the framework does not deal with other underlying inequalities, such as class and race. Women cannot be considered as a homogeneous category, who all share the same needs. In fact, women have interests and needs associated with other aspects of their identity – for example, class, age, or disability. A female domestic worker will have needs

which are not shared with her female employer. The term 'gender needs' should not, therefore, be used synonymously with 'women's needs'; in practice, this confusion often occurs.

Autonomy, not overwork or the triple role may be women's main concern
In some cases, the key issue for women is not the problem of balancing their different roles, but the fact that their roles are extremely restricted. In some cases, women have no 'community role' because they live in seclusion and are unable to mix in the community; in other cases, they are excluded from productive work.

Division between strategic and practical is artificial
Some people argue that the clear division between practical and strategic needs or interests is unhelpful, as in most cases there is a continuum from practical to strategic. For instance, is education a practical or strategic issue? The important thing is to think about how you can meet immediate and urgent needs in such a way as to begin challenging gender inequalities. Some people prefer Kate Young's (1987) idea of transformatory potential to that of strategic and practical needs. This concept advocates that women themselves examine their practical needs and look for ways of striving to meet them which have 'the capacity or potential for questioning, undermining, or transforming gender relations and the structure of subordination.' (Young, 1987).

Others argue that all practical interventions affect women's power and status, even when this is not factored into the planning process or recognised by those involved in the project (Longwe 1994). It is therefore dangerous to assume that practical and strategic are separate areas of interest.

Ignores men as 'gendered' beings
Moser's definition of strategic gender needs leads users to consider these for women only. Some people believe that this makes the concept powerful, because it underlines that women are the subordinated sex in a patriarchal system. Others believe that we need to broaden the concept to one which includes men's strategic gender interests, since men have very strong vested interests in any process of change, or in maintaining the status quo. Examining these will help us understand better how to work with men, and to anticipate where, and how, they may resist women's empowerment.

The adaptation of Moser's work by the DPU has redefined 'gender needs' in its Web of Institutionalisation to include men's practical and strategic gender needs. See Appendix (p 123) for definitions.

Change over time is not examined as a variable

Policy approaches may be misunderstood as clear-cut categories
The policy approaches characterised by Moser are sometimes criticised as false dichotomies, because there have been many variations. Although Moser

does point out that her categorisation should only be seen as showing the 'pure' version of each policy approach, her neat (but deliberately simplified) classification can lead to the trap of summing up an intervention in terms of a policy approach, without looking closely enough at the details. For instance, an intervention providing services to support women's reproductive role does not necessarily use a welfare approach – it may be part of a well thought-out strategy of transformation.

New policy approaches need to be developed and conceptualised

The characterisation of policy approaches in the Moser Framework is a powerful tool both for examining the history of development, and for examining the underlying goals and assumptions of existing policy and project interventions. However, although we need to be aware of past approaches and their influence on our current thinking, we must also be ready to explore new approaches as appropriate to given contexts. Some would argue that there is a danger that people will try to work too much within the given approaches, rather than recognising how dynamic policy is, and should be.

Some users said they find it more useful simply to work with the distinction between Women in Development (WID) and Gender and Development (GAD) as approaches.

May encounter strong resistance

The goal of gender planning in the Moser Framework is the 'emancipation of women from their subordination'. Strong resistance will exist where development workers do not accept this as a legitimate aim.

Further reading

Part of the Moser framework was first outlined in Caroline Moser and Caren Levy (1986) 'A Theory and Method of Gender Planning – Meeting Women's Practical and Strategic Needs', DPU Gender and Planning Working Paper No. 11, published by the Development Planning Unit, London.

Caroline Moser's more recent book, *Gender Planning in Development: Theory, Practice and Training*, Routledge, London, 1993, is worth reading for an extremely comprehensive description of the background and application of the framework.

An interesting commentary from users of the Moser Framework (quoted from in the above Commentary) can be found in Kabeer, N (1994) *Reversed Realities: Gender Hierarchies in Development Thought*, Verso, London.

2.4 | Gender Analysis Matrix (GAM)

Background

The Gender Analysis Matrix (GAM) was developed by Rani Parker,[8] in collaboration with development practitioners working for a Middle Eastern NGO. They expressed a need for a framework appropriate to their grassroots work. As a result, the GAM is very much influenced by the reality and ideology of participatory planning; it can also accommodate the constraints imposed by shortage of funding and time, illiteracy, and insufficient or non-existent quantitative data on gender roles.

All the information in this section, including the case study, comes from *Another Point of View: A Manual on Gender Analysis Training for Grassroots Workers*, by A. Rani Parker, published by UNIFEM in 1993. A reprint is available from Women, Ink. Publishers, New York.

Aims of the framework

The GAM aims to help determine the different impact development interventions have on women and men, by providing a community-based technique for identifying and analysing gender differences. The GAM is a transformatory tool, in that its use is intended to initiate a process of analysis by community members themselves. It encourages the community to identify and constructively challenge their assumptions about gender roles.

The framework

The GAM is based on the following principles:

- All requisite knowledge for gender analysis exists among the people whose lives are the subject of the analysis.

- Gender analysis does not require the technical expertise of those outside the community, except as facilitators.

- Gender analysis cannot promote transformation unless it is carried out by the people being analysed. (Parker 1993, 2)

The GAM is filled in by a group within the community which, preferably, should include women and men in equal numbers. The GAM can be used at different stages in the project cycle, to assess both the potential and the actual impact of an intervention on the community's gender relations. The objectives at each stage are as follows: 'At the planning stage to determine whether potential gender effects are desirable and consistent with programme goals; at the design stages where gender considerations may change the design of the project; or during monitoring and evaluation stages, to address broader programme impacts'. (Parker 1993, 29)

The GAM features two main concepts on a matrix which focuses on the impact of a development intervention.

Example of GAM				
	Labour	**Time**	**Resources**	**Culture**
Women				
Men				
Household				
Community				

Source: Parker 1993

GAM Tool 1: Analysis at four 'levels' of society

The GAM analyses the impact of development interventions at four levels: women, men, households, and community. Other levels (depending on the project goals and the community in question) such as age group, class, ethnic group, and so on, can be added as appropriate. The four main categories which appear vertically on the GAM matrix are defined below.

Women: This refers to women of all ages who are in the target group (if the target group includes women), or to all women in the community.

Men: This refers to men of all ages who are in the target group (if the target group includes men), or to all men in the community.

Household: This refers to all women, men, and children living together, even if they are not part of one nuclear family. Although the type of household may vary even within the same community, people always know what constitutes their 'household' or 'family'. Their own definition or unit of analysis should be used for this level in the GAM.

Community: This refers to everyone within the project area. The purpose of this level is to extend the analysis beyond the family. However, communities are complex and usually comprise a number of different groups of people with different interests. So if a clearly defined 'community' is not meaningful in the context of the project, this level of analysis may be eliminated. (Parker 1993)

GAM Tool 2: Analysis of four kinds of impact

The GAM looks at impact on four areas: labour, time, resources (considering both access and control), and socio-cultural factors. These categories appear horizontally on the GAM matrix.

Labour: This refers to changes in tasks (for example, fetching water from the river), the level of skill required (skilled or unskilled, formal education, training), and labour capacity (How many people carry out a task, and how much can they do? Is it necessary to hire labour, or can members of the household do the work?).

Time: This refers to changes in the amount of time (three hours, four days, and so on) it takes to carry out the task associated with the project or activity.

Resources: This category refers to the changes in access to resources (income, land, and credit) as a consequence of the project, and the extent of control over changes in resources (more or less) for each group analysed.

Socio-cultural factors: This refers to changes in social aspects of the participants' lives (including changes in gender roles or status) as a result of the project. (Parker 1993)

Using the GAM

The GAM is used with groups of community members (with equal representation of women and men), facilitated by a development worker. Over time, it is hoped that community members themselves will facilitate the process, but Rani Parker points out that in the early stages, an experienced facilitator is needed. The analysis is always done by the group.

It is intended that the analysis in the GAM should be reviewed and revised once a month for the first three months, and once every three months thereafter. Every box should be verified on each review of the GAM. Unexpected results, as well as expected ones, must be added to the matrix.

When the GAM has been filled in, the group discusses the findings by asking the following questions.

- Are the effects listed on the GAM desirable? Are they consistent with the programme's goals?

- How is the intervention affecting those who do not participate?
- Which results are unexpected? (These will appear on GAMs filled in during and after implementation.)

After the boxes have been filled in with the changes brought about by the project, group members should go back to the matrix and add the following:

- a plus sign (+) if the outcome is consistent with project goals;
- a minus sign (-) if the outcome is contrary to project goals;
- a question mark (?) if they are unsure whether it is consistent or contrary.

These signs are intended to give a picture of the different effects of the intervention; they are not intended to be added up in an effort to determine its net effect. This would over-simplify the picture of complex reality, and mis-represent the mix of positive and negative effects which all interventions have.

The GAM is intended to be used in addition to other standard tools of analysis such as monitoring tools, needs assessments, and so on.

Case study of GAM: Potable water in Ouled Hamouda

This case study focuses on development work in a community of 110 families called Ouled Hamouda, in the town of Makhtar in Western Tunisia. Here, the women had to walk two kilometres down a very steep, muddy path to get water. Twice each day, they filled their cans with water and carried the 20 litre cans on their backs up the steep hill. Even pregnant or sick woman did this, or those carrying their little children who could not be left behind alone in the house.

The Tunisian Foundation for Community Development (le Fondation Tunisienne pour le Developpement Communautaire/ FTDC) organises periodic development meetings in each of the 22 communities where it works. During these meetings, the community identifies problems, classifies, and prioritises these, identifies which projects would address problems, and discusses what contribution the community can make to the projects. Contributions can be in cash, kind, or labour.

In Ouled Hamouda, where the FTDC had worked for seven years, the women rated their difficulty in getting water as their biggest problem. Men, who never fetch water, rated this problem as their fifth priority. Traditionally, men, not women, construct wells. The use of the Gender Analysis Matrix in Ouled Hamouda enabled the men to understand the potential impact of addressing this problem at all four levels identified in the matrix. After completing the matrix, both women and men classified the water project as their first priority.

A committee for potable water was created, which included women and men selected by the community. A well was constructed only 300 metres away from people's homes, and equipped with a motor pump that ejected water into a large, well-constructed cistern. Today the water project is completed and potable water is easily accessible to everyone in the community.

Initial Gender Analysis Matrix from Ouled Hamouda

This matrix represents the combined views of men and women in Ouled Hamouda. It represents their expectations of the impact of a project to bring potable water to the village. It enabled men and women to think through the importance and desirability of such a project. The pluses and minuses were added afterwards; a plus if the change was consistent with the project goal, a minus if it was not.

Using the GAM: Project objectives in Ouled Hamouda				
	Labour	**Time**	**Resources**	**Culture**
Women	+ Don't need to carry big cans of water + No fears about personal security	+ Save time + Have more time with children	- Must pay for water + Can have home garden or other small projects	- Responsibility of paying for water + Opportunity to participate in community project
Men	- A lot of work, difficult work + Learn new skills for work outside the community	- Takes a lot more time to build, dig, etc + Can stay home with family while working	+ Portable water is available + Improved nutrition	+ Don't have to worry as much about the family when away
Household	+ Women feel more secure when fetching water - can leave child at home + New activity for entire family	+ Women can give more time to child care	+ Easy access to potable water + Improved nutrition and better health	+ New activity for children - they can help their mother
Community	+ Establish Committee for Potable Water + Learn about services provided by government	- Less free time for leisure - Many more community meetings to attend	+ More potable water available for all	+ Clean environment + Prestige for the community

Source: Parker 1993, 52.

Questions arising from the matrix, and answers given in discussion:

- Are the effects listed above desirable and consistent with programme goals?
  Yes.

- How will this activity affect those who do not participate?
  All community members will benefit from better access to potable water.

- Were there unexpected results, to be identified during implementation:
  There were some unexpected results, which are included in the next section.
  (Parker 1992, 52)

Changes in Ouled Hamouda following the project

- The new water source provided potable water.

- Men became more aware of the burden of women's labour.

- Although the women had assumed that they would have to pay for the water, the men paid for it, because the job of collecting payments fell to a male member of the committee.

- Some aspects of existing gender relations were reinforced: for example, the receiving and handling of money remained in the men's hands. Although a woman was assigned to check water usage and to ensure that everything worked, the men actually came in and carried out the repairs.

- Once the project was completed, men and children began to fetch water, changing the traditional gender division of labour for this task.

- Systems of organisation within the community were strengthened as systems for collecting payments for water usage were developed. The community determined the charges for water usage; they agreed that four families would be allowed to use the water free of charge, because they could not afford to pay for it.

- The new water source provided greater personal security for women. Also, since the well was close by, women were able to leave small children at home while they went to fetch water.

- Men spent more time at home during the project construction phase and later were able to market their skills in water-system construction and maintenance.

- The committee used to attend a district meeting at which men from other communities had ridiculed the men of Ouled Hamouda because there were so many women participating in the decision-making. This also has changed, and although there are still not many women on committees, the women on the Ouled Hamouda committee are increasingly becoming accepted in their new roles of leadership. (Parker 1993, 53)

Commentary on GAM

Uses

A participatory planning tool

The GAM is expressly designed for planning, designing, monitoring, and evaluating projects at a community level.

Useful for transformatory gender training

The GAM is a tool with a high potential for raising awareness of women's subordination as a result of unequal gender relations, so it is appropriate for use in transformatory gender training.

Purpose-designed training manual

The manual outlining the use of the GAM has been specifically designed for training purposes and includes a training methodology.

Why it appeals

Designed specifically for community-based development workers

The framework was specifically developed to fit in the reality of community-based development workers: it is accessible, flexible, and designed to accommodate changes over time, including those which are unexpected.

Simple and systematic; uses familiar categories and concepts

GAM is simple and systematic. GAM does not rely on unique or new concepts, but instead employs ones familiar to gender and development researchers and workers. Others who encounter these concepts and categories for the first time when using GAM can transfer them to other gender and development work.

Transformatory as well as technical

The GAM is designed to initiate a learning process. Parker claims that over time, the likelihood of changes favouring gender equity is increased. This is borne out by one user who sees the GAM as a useful tool for gender training because it raises consciousness about gender inequalities through the design of the categories of analysis. Because they move from practical issues to cultural change, participants cannot avoid making the links between practical impact and intangible changes at a cultural and ideological level. The use of the GAM means that transformatory work takes place simultaneously to the acquisition of practical skills.

Fosters 'bottom-up' analysis through community participation

The process of analysis should fully involve the people who are the subjects of the analysis, drawing on, and valueing, the group's diverse strengths and perspectives, rather than relying on individual expertise. The GAM enables members of the community to articulate a full range of expectations concerning a particular project.

Considers gender relations between women and men, as well as examining what each category experiences separately

The use of both the categories of household and community, as well as of women and men is one way of trying to draw out the connectedness of gender relations. It helps move gender and development workers away from a tendency to see men and women as separate, homogeneous groups, which can be considered in isolation from each other. One user comments that the inclusion of men gains the confidence of male participants in a gender training workshop since they no longer see facilitators 'talking about gender, but focusing on women only'.

Levels of analysis can be added to in order to suit particular interventions

The levels of analysis can incorporate various groups within the community; for example, a project targeting girl children can include them as a category.

Includes intangible resources.

In addition to labour and resources, GAM also highlights time and socio-political issues.

Can be used to capture changes over time

A single use of the GAM will provide only a 'snapshot' of one particular moment in a project's life. However, by repeating the GAM process, the tool can be used to follow changes over time. When complete, the GAMs filled in over the duration of a project can provide a dynamic overview of the negative and positive effects of a single project/ programme on a community.

Helps anticipate resistance, and encourages consideration of what support should be offered for those at risk

The participatory process which the GAM insists on enables all concerned, from funding agencies to the community, to anticipate the resistance that the project or programme might meet from participants and non-participants. One user comments that this is invaluable for projects where women 'beneficiaries' need to be aware that they may be subject to violence from men, as a result of challenging gender relations. Implementing agencies must include in their plans the kinds of support which groups who would be under threat have a right to be offered.

Includes men as gendered beings, so can be used in interventions which target men

The levels of analysis include men as well as women, and therefore the framework can be used in situations where men or boys are the target of a development intervention, due to their particular experience of the gender division of labour and power (for example, work with ex-combatants, child miners, in anti-violence projects, and so on). Caroline Sweetman, of Oxfam GB, reports that gender training with male participants was made easier by the inclusion of the category of men, because it overcame men's resistance. One participant told her 'we usually hear facilitators talking about gender but focusing on women only'.

Can be used for participatory impact assessment
The GAM is a very useful tool for impact assessment. It is an effective way of bringing out local impact indicators, building on the project members' own analysis.

Quick data gathering
Filling in a GAM can be a relatively quick way of gathering complex and rich data. According to the author, the completion of a GAM takes two to four hours, especially during the first few analyses.

Potential limitations

Needs a good facilitator
For the analysis to be effective, a good facilitator is required. When the GAM is first introduced, or when no literate facilitator can be found within the community, facilitation will be needed from outside the community.

Some factors can get lost because categories have many aspects
The facilitator must take care to remember and to remind everyone in the group that each category of analysis incorporates many aspects, not just the most obvious ones. For example, 'labour' includes skills as well as training, 'resources' must differentiate between access and control, and the category 'cultural factors' can include everything that is done to continue and/ or expand existing social networks.

Requires careful repetition in order to consider change over time
The matrix requires repetition of the analysis over time. Once begun, the process must be continued to ensure that negative perceptions and stereotypes about gender roles are challenged.

Does not seek out the most vulnerable community members
Although the GAM can be expanded to consider specific inequalities which cross-cut gender divisions, such as ethnicity, it does not explicitly differentiate which men, and which women, are most likely to experience negative or positive impacts. Finding this out must be seen by the facilitators as a crucial part of their role. An adaptation is to add 'Which women, which men' in large letters under the matrix.

Excludes macro- and institutional analysis
The GAM framework does not consider the potentials offered and the constraints imposed by either the implementing agencies or external forces beyond the community.

Difficulties defining a community

It is sometimes difficult to define who is actually participating in the project, or who should be deemed as the community.

Subordination is often not explicit

Participatory methods, including the GAM, give scope to explore women's perspectives. However, there is a danger that the GAM can lead to a false consensus and false confidence that women have taken an equal part in defining the future. Where women's views have previously been silenced, the process of filling in the GAM may not be enough to capture their perspectives of the complex links between their problems and their subordinate status. It is likely that much time must be spent with women to find ways of articulating issues which they consider important.

While the GAM is designed for use with mixed groups, there may be times when it is better to use it with women-only or men-only groups, or with groups of young women and older women separately, depending on the context.

Risk of misleading outcomes due to power relations between funders and community members

As with all participatory methods, there is a risk of misleading outcomes, because community members may resist discussing all issues freely; for example, negative aspects of the project may not be discussed for fear of funding being refused. It is important that the community has trust in the process and in the implementing agencies.

Further reading

The Gender Analysis Matrix is presented in a very user-friendly training manual: *Another point of view: A manual on gender analysis training for grassroots workers*, A Rani Parker, published by UNIFEM, 1993, and reprinted by Women's Ink., New York, 1998. The manual has been specifically designed for training purposes and includes a training methodology; a section for the audience to assess for themselves the uses and limitations of the framework; and materials which can be reproduced for handouts.

2.5 | Capacities and Vulnerabilities Analysis Framework

'Development is a process by which vulnerabilities are reduced and capacities are increased.' (Anderson and Woodrow 1989, 12).

Background

The Capacities and Vulnerabilities Analysis (CVA), like the People-Oriented Analytical Framework, was designed specifically for use in humanitarian interventions, and for disaster preparedness.

However, unlike the POP Framework, the CVA is not grounded in a single agency's experience of relief work. Rather, it resulted from a research project, the International Relief and Development Project at Harvard University, which examined 30 case studies of NGOs responding to various disaster situations around the world. Some of the people who were involved in designing the framework also developed the Harvard Analytical Framework.

Information here is adapted from the book by Anderson M, Woodrow P, *Rising from the Ashes: Development Strategies in Times of Disaster*, Westview Press, Boulder and San Francisco, and UNESCO, Paris 1989. Copyright 1998 by Lynne Rienner Publishers, Inc. Used with permission of the publisher.

Aims of the Framework

The CVA was designed to help outside agencies plan aid in emergencies, in such a way that interventions meet immediate needs, and at the same time build on the strengths of people and their efforts to achieve long-term social and economic development.

The Framework

CVA is based on the central idea that people's existing strengths (or capacities) and weaknesses (or vulnerabilities) determine the impact that a crisis has on them, as well as the way they respond to the crisis. A crisis becomes a disaster when it outstrips a society's capacity to cope In the long term, emergency interventions should aim to increase people's capacities, and reduce their vulnerabilities. As such, CVA is a developmental approach to relief in emergencies.

In the following, the concepts of capacities and vulnerabilities are defined.

Capacities: This term describes the existing strengths of individuals and social groups. They are related to people's material and physical resources, their social resources, and their beliefs and attitudes. Capacities are built over time and determine people's ability to cope with crisis and recover from it.

Vulnerabilities: These are the long-term factors which weaken people's ability to cope with the sudden onset of disaster, or with drawn-out emergencies. They also make people more susceptible to disasters. Vulnerabilities exist before disasters, contribute to their severity, make effective disaster response harder, and continue after the disaster.

The concept of vulnerabilities in the CVA framework is very different from the concept of needs as used in a disaster context. Needs here are not used in the sense of practical and strategic gender needs; they are understood as 'immediate requirements for survival or recovery from crisis' (Anderson and Woodrow 1989, 10). Therefore immediate needs are often addressed by short-term, practical interventions (such as relief food). Addressing vulnerabilities, in contrast, requires the long-term strategic solutions which are part of development work.

For instance, those who experience regular mudslides in an urban area may have needs for temporary shelters and medical attention. On the other hand, their vulnerabilities are linked to those factors which directly contribute to the suffering caused by the mudslide (crowding, building homes on unstable land) and to others which indirectly affect the community's ability to respond to serious crisis (rural-to-urban migration, lack of government legislation on building codes, absence of strong community organisations) (Anderson and Woodrow 1989, 10).

CVA Tool 1: Categories of capacities and vulnerabilities

The CVA distinguishes between three categories of capacities and vulnerabilities, using an analysis matrix. The three categories used are physical, social, and motivational capacities and vulnerabilities.

Physical or material capacities and vulnerabilities: These include features of the climate, land, and environment where people live, or lived before the crisis; their health, skills, their work; their housing, technologies, water and food supply; their access to capital and other assets. All of these will be different for women and for men. While women and men suffer material deprivation during crisis, they always have some resources left, including skills and possibly goods. These are capacities upon which agencies can build.

The CVA encourages users to ask two main questions.

- What were/ are the ways in which men and women in the community were/ are physically or materially vulnerable?

- What productive resources, skills, and hazards existed/ exist? Who (men and/ or women) had/ have access and control over these resources?

Social or organisational capacities and vulnerabilities: This category refers to the social fabric of a community, and includes the formal political structures and the informal systems through which people make decisions, establish leadership, or organise various social and economic activities. Social systems include family and community systems, and decision-making patterns within the family and between families.

Gender analysis in this category is crucial, because women's and men's roles in these various forms of organisation differ widely. Decision-making in social groups may exclude women, or women may have well-developed systems for exchanging labour and goods. Divisions on the basis of gender, race, class, or ethnicity, can weaken the social fabric of a group, and increase its vulnerability.

CVA asks users to consider:

- What was the social structure of the community before the disaster, and how did it serve them in the face of this disaster?

- What has been the impact of the disaster on social organisation?

- What is the level and quality of participation in these structures?

Motivational and attitudinal capacities and vulnerabilities: These include cultural and psychological factors which may be based on religion, on the community's history of crisis, on their expectation of emergency relief. Crisis can be a catalyst for extraordinary efforts by communities, but when people feel victimised and dependent, they may become fatalistic and passive, and suffer a decrease in their capacities to cope with and recover from the situation. Their vulnerabilities can be increased by inappropriate relief aid, which does not build on people's own abilities, develop their confidence, or offer them opportunities for change.

CVA encourages users to ask:

- How do men and women in the community view themselves, and their ability to deal effectively with their social/ political environment?

- What were people's beliefs and motivations before the disaster and how has the disaster affected them? This includes beliefs about gender roles and relations.

- Do people feel they have the ability to shape their lives? Do men and women feel they have the same ability?

Example of the Capacities and Vulnerabilities Analysis Matrix		
	Vulnerabilities	**Capacities**
Physical/ material What productive resources, skills, and hazards exist?		
Social/ organisational What are the relationships between people? What are their organisational structures?		
Motivational/ attitudinal How does the community view its ability to create change?		
'Development is the process by which vulnerabilities are reduced and capacities increased.'		

Source: Anderson and Woodrow 1989, 12

CVA Tool 2: Additional dimensions of 'complex reality'
In order to make the CVA matrix reflect reality's complexity, five other dimensions must be added to the analysis.

Disaggregation of communities by gender
Capacities, vulnerabilities, and needs are differentiated by gender. Women and men experience crisis differently, according to their gender roles. They have different needs and interests. Women, by virtue of their lower economic, social, and political status, tend to be more vulnerable to crisis. They may also be more open to change – and gender roles can change rapidly as a result of emergencies. CVA enables these forms of social differentiation to be taken into account and mapped out on the matrix (see overleaf, top table).

Disaggregation according to other dimensions of social relations
A community can also be analysed according to other factors which stratify it: by the level of wealth (see overleaf, bottom table), by political affiliation, by ethnic or language groups, by age, and so on. The question always of who reveals how different people and groups are differently affected by crisis and interventions.

Example of CVA Matrix disaggregated by gender

	Vulnerabilities		Capacities	
	Women	Men	Women	Men
Physical/material				
Social/organisational				
Motivational/attitudinal				

Source: Anderson and Woodrow 1989, 16

Example of CVA Matrix disaggregated by economic class

	Vulnerabilities			Capacities		
	Rich	Middle	Poor	Rich	Middle	Poor
Physical/material						
Social/organisational						
Motivational/attitudinal						

Source: Anderson and Woodrow 1989, 16

Change over time

Societies are dynamic, and change over time. The CVA Matrix only provides a snapshot of a given moment. However, it can be used repeatedly – for example, before an intervention and after – to examine social change and to evaluate impact. In particular, the CVA Matrix can be used to assess change in gender relations as a result of an emergency, and of agency interventions.

'Interactions' between categories of analysis

There is constant interaction between the categories of analysis used in CVA. Different categories of vulnerabilities and capacities are related to each other, and changes in one will have an impact on the others. For example, increasing people's social organisations may reduce their vulnerability to material loss, and also increase group confidence.

Analysis at different scales and levels of society

CVA can be applied to small villages and neighbourhoods, to larger districts, to whole nations, and even to regions. As the scale of application increases, the factors examined become less precisely defined; but one can still assess both the disaster proneness and the development potential at each level.

There are also interactions between different levels of society. Various social groups are affected differently by policies and events at the regional, national, and international level. Applying CVA to different levels can help you assess what the links between the different levels are (Anderson and Woodrow 1989, 16).

Case study on CVA: Gender and vulnerability among refugees from Sierra Leone in Guinea

This case study is based on the work of Fiona Gell, then an advisor in Oxfam GB's Emergencies Department.

Following a rebel attack in the north of Sierra Leone at the beginning of 1995, many refugees fled across the border to south-western Guinea. An estimated 20,000 refugees sheltered in local towns and villages, receiving food and shelter from the host population. The refugees were a mix of different ethnicities, and had fled from different parts of Sierra Leone. Some were agriculturalists, while others had lived in cities. The majority belonged to an ethnic group which spans the Sierra Leone-Guinea border.

During the summer, UNHCR staff encouraged the refugees to construct houses on seven sites, and a re-registration of refugees followed. Oxfam GB assisted with emergency water provision, and a sanitation and community-health programme. This involved supporting existing health posts in the refugee-affected area. UNHCR provided food, household items, clothes, and tools for house construction for those living on the sites. Refugees are now increasingly requesting assistance for programmes supporting self-reliance and education.

Fiona Gell, a gender and representation adviser for Oxfam's emergency programmes, spent two months in south-western Guinea investigating issues of gender and vulnerability within the refugee population, using participatory rural appraisal exercises and holding discussions with Oxfam's community health supervisors and representatives of the UNHCR, NGOs, local government and community organisations. We first list some highlights from her findings on the refugees' physical and material capacities and vulnerabilities below, and then present a completed CVA matrix, which sums up these issues and also features the social/ organisational and motivational/ attitudinal aspects of her research.

Physical/material vulnerabilities

- Although UNHCR provided all refugees with a general monthly food ration, they assumed that families were able to supplement their diet independently, which is normally the case. Those who found this particularly hard included female-headed households, unaccompanied elderly persons, people with disabilities, and urban people who had trading skills but who no longer had access to start-up capital.

- There was a high level of disease during the rainy season, when there is also scarce food and very little money.

- Female-headed households faced particular difficulties in registration:
  - some had registered their families in the name of absent men, and were unable to re-register precisely because these men were absent;
  - some were pushed out of line and then did not register because they lacked the time to queue again;
  - some were unable to register because they were attending a sick child in hospital.

- Certain female-headed households, unaccompanied elderly people, and heads of household with disabilities were unable to access adult male labour to construct houses on site and thus qualify for registration.

- Female heads of household had fewer opportunities to generate income than male heads, mainly because of domestic responsibilities. The pressure to construct a house meant that many women sold large quantities of their food rations to buy labour, or took out loans against the next food ration, thus depleting the family's already minimal food supply.

- A number of people with disabilities such as deafness or mental illness were unaware of the importance of registration.

- Allusions were also made to women succumbing to sexual coercion to access labour.

- Some female-headed households also complained of not getting equal access to tools for house construction. Tools were distributed to groups of five families, and distribution was typically dominated by men.

- Some people with disabilities such as leprosy had trouble getting food during distribution.

- Refugees who were originally urban traders had little experience of agriculture, house- and latrine-construction, and were unaccustomed to the rigours of rural life.

Physical/material capacities

- UNHCR supplied monthly food rations.

- Refugees generated income by selling maize rations, blankets, and so on.

- Both women and men had found work on local farms as day labourers; some had made crop-sharing arrangements; where there were rivers, men had found work as fishers.

- Some refugees had owned land in the area for many years as well as in their home villages. Some had found land nearby (on either side of the border), which they returned to frequently. Those with land on Sierra Leone's side of the border returned to the camps at night for security.

- Many people, particularly those women who had traditionally been traders, managed to generate a small income by trading in small items. Children were also involved in trade.

- Women with relatives among the host population had access to capital.

- Women's skills included soap-making, baking, textile-dyeing, petty trading, agriculture (growing groundnuts, rice, and vegetables); they also worked as teachers, traditional birth attendants, and community workers.

- Five of Oxfam's community-health supervisors were trained teachers who had been trained in counselling children.

- Palm wine was tapped by men from ethnic groups which are more permissive about alcohol consumption.

- Female-headed households were potentially able to exchange labour for male labour.

- Some women who headed households had taken on traditionally male roles, while others had not.

Social/ organisational vulnerabilities

- 27% of households were headed by women whose husbands had either been killed by the rebels or were living elsewhere. While some female-headed households adapted to the new conditions by changing their traditional role, others were evidently unable to cope adequately.

- Less favoured wives in polygamous marriages often faced similar problems to female-headed households.

- Refugees who were originally traders were less likely to have kinship networks in the new settlement areas. Refugees arrived in the area after having walked long distances, physically and psychologically exhausted. In addition, many of them did not speak the local language.

- The Red Cross expressed concern about child trafficking.

- Prostitution was common.

Social/ organisational capacities

- Many refugees had strong kinship ties across the border and/ or owned land on both sides of the border. This often meant that local families offered food and shelter in return for agricultural and domestic work; many refugees were loaned a plot of land for cultivation. With the move to the refugee sites, some of the refugees had managed to maintain these economic ties.

- No unaccompanied children were identified, and orphans had been taken in by other families. Informal reports suggest that orphans fare less well during food shortages.

- The population was extremely mobile as families pursued several survival strategies at any one time. Many of the families who owned land close to the border in Sierra Leone left some members behind on the farm to guard the property and start farming. Other family members returned daily to help on the land. A few family members, often the wife and a few children, would stay at the refugee site to maintain a presence and guard the house.

- The women in some ethnic groups for women form groups to work small areas of donated land, according to tradition.

- There were women's organisations among the host population which ran income-generation and rice and vegetable production schemes. These had stated their willingness to share their skills with refugee women.

- Refugee committees existed.

Motivational/attitudinal vulnerabilities

- Many refugees, particularly women, had relatives who were tortured, killed, or taken by the rebels, and many had witnessed horrific atrocities. Many had fled several times, and did not know whether their relatives were dead or alive. Most of the refugees seemed to be coping quietly with the enormous subsequent psychological stress, but a few had evidently developed symptoms of mental illness.

Motivational/attitudinal capacities

- The combination of survival strategies (such as returning across the border to work on their old farms at the same time as registering on the refugee sites) seemed to allow families to maintain some level of independence, while also making sure they would remain eligible for external assistance (such as food distribution) which would be necessary in the case of further attacks and insecurity.

- The types of support refugees asked for most were education and constructive play for the children; income generation for adults; and co-operative commercial ventures to rebuild social networks broken down by dispersal and flight. Assistance with the tracing of missing family members would help restore some sense of hope in the future.

- There was a wealth of primary and secondary school teachers within the refugee population. Some refugees had set up schools where teachers worked without pay.

Recommendations

Following Fiona Gell's survey and her analysis of the refugee community's capacities and vulnerabilities, she made a number of recommendations including those below.

To combat the vulnerabilities she advised:

- to install a system for the registration of those refugees who were missed in the previous registration, or who had recently arrived;

- to supplement the diet of those physically vulnerable (such as children under five or lactating mothers) or vulnerable for socio-economic reasons (such as single parent families or unaccompanied elderly persons);

- to encourage the full representation of those people with particular vulnerabilities on existing refugee committees;

- to explore some form of psycho-social support for those individuals who were unable to cope with their severely distressing experiences;

- to request the services of the International Committee of the Red Cross for the tracing of relatives, as much of the stress refugees suffered related to the disappearance of family members.

To build on capacities, Fiona Gell recommended:

- to promote income-generation schemes for those unable to raise income or construct houses, such as those from cities who had no kinship ties with the settled region, or female-headed households. (Proposals had already been made for such small business programmes, individual skills had been identified, and work groups organised.)

- to use the refugee committees actively to find out about the views of all sectors of the refugee population.

- to explore how psycho-social support could be provided using resources within the community, perhaps starting with Oxfam's community-health supervisors, who were already trained in counselling children.

- To build on the fact that Oxfam's community-health supervisors and their team of health workers could give advice on what kind of support the most vulnerable families needed, as well as on who were the most capable refugees for co-ordinating self-reliance programmes.

Using the CVA Matrix: refugees in Sierra Leone

	Vulnerabilities	Capacities
Physical/ material What productive resources, skills, and hazards exist?	Female heads of households unable to access male labour to construct camp houses; thus not eligible to receive food rations. As a consequence, many women: • are coerced into giving sexual favours to access male labour; • are forced into taking out loans against next food ration, leading to debt cycle; • are involved in prostitution in urban host communities.	Women's skills include: • income-generation (making soap, baking, dyeing textile, petty trading); • agriculture (groundnuts, rice, and vegetables); • vocational work (teachers, traditional birth attendants, community workers)
Social/ organisational What are the relationships between people? What are their organisational structures?	• 27% of households led by a woman (husbands killed, disappeared or away searching for work); • Distribution of tools in camp dominated by men; female heads of households do no have full access.	• Traditional practice of women forming groups to work small areas of donated land; • Close kinship ties between refugees and host communities allow exchange of food, shelter, and land for labour; • Labour exchanges between men and women enable female-headed households to access male labour for house-building.
Motivational/ attitudinal How does the community view its ability to create change?	• Morale very low on arrival at camp among people who fled rebel fighters several times, following repeated attacks, • Many women who lost husbands and children to the rebels particularly affected.	After a time, refugees developed survival strategies to maximise opportunity to earn an income: • women and children remained in camp; • young men returned to Sierra Leone to guard the land and start farming.

Commentary on CVA

Uses

In emergencies and for development work
The CVA was designed for use in humanitarian interventions and so is especially useful in disaster relief. However, it is also a useful tool in development work, particularly for communities in vulnerable areas or those affected by chronic crises.

As a planning and assessment tool
CVA can be used to plan responses. In addition, by applying it over time, it can be used to assess change, particularly change brought about in gender relations as the result of an emergency, or of agency interventions.

Useful at different levels
CVA can be used at different levels - from the community to the national, regional, and even international level, thus enabling researchers to assess the links between the different levels.

Why it appeals

'Maps' complexity
CVA helps to chart a complex real situation, to highlight its crucial factors, and to illustrate the relationships between factors which matter most to project effectiveness.

Can be used at different stages
The CVA model is flexible and can be used before, during, and after a disaster, major change, or intervention.

Encourages a long-term perspective
CVA encourages a combination of long-term and short-term perspectives and strategies, to ensure that vulnerabilities are reduced and capacities improved.

Examines social interactions and the psychological realm
The CVA Framework attempts to ensure that an NGO will not only concentrate on material things. It gives prominence to the social interactions within a community, such as social cohesion and leadership, highlighting that these can be a resource or a hindrance. It also emphasises the psychological realm, and is able to examine emotions such as loss of hope in the future. Motivation and attitudes are seen as crucial resources or barriers, and interventions designed with CVA should take these into account. In some cases, responses directly address them. For example, in the Philippines, agencies have undertaken work with children suffering stress after typhoons.

Simple, but not simplistic
The CVA framework is relatively simple to understand and use; yet it is not over-simplistic.

Includes other forms of inequality
The CVA matrix model can be adapted to take into account all forms of social differentiation, such as gender, class, caste, age, race, ethnicity, and so on.

Can be adapted for macro-level analysis
The CVA is easier to adapt to macro-analysis than the Harvard Analytical Framework. It is important for researchers and planners to look beyond the community experiencing crisis (using the concept of scales or levels), to see the constraints and opportunities for promoting gender equality in the wider context (the international community, the state, the market, and so on) and within the implementing agencies.

Challenges the status quo
Analysing a community's capacities vulnerabilities using this framework can help to counter arguments that oppressive social relationships within the community should not be challenged after a crisis, but that a return to the former state of affairs should be sought. The long-term factors which determine a community's response to crisis (including gender relations) must be addressed, and changed, in order to ensure recovery and prevent another crisis.

Highlights people's capacities, as well as their vulnerabilities
By examining capacities, the CVA can help agencies and those experiencing disaster to work against any tendency to see crisis primarily in terms of 'victims' and 'needs'.

Potential limitations

Possible to exclude a gender analysis
It is very easy to use the CVA Framework and to still exclude gender issues, thus creating gender-blind analyses and responses. It is crucial that the analysis disaggregates vulnerabilities and capacities by gender, and includes an explicit analysis of power relations between men and women.

Tahmina Rahman, a gender specialist who has worked in emergency situations, argues that an effective way of doing this is to first carry out a participatory analysis with community members, using the Harvard Analytical Framework or POP. She argues that either of these works well with the CVA; they provide a strong base of gender-disaggregated data on which to build a CVA, and the CVA then draws out the relationships between different groups, counter-balancing the tendency of the Harvard Framework and POP to see women and men separately.

Does not include an explicit agenda for women's empowerment
Although the concepts of capacities and vulnerabilities can be powerful when considering gender inequalities, the CVA Framework is not designed

specifically to promote women's empowerment. If you plan to use it for gender-redistributive planning, it is crucial that you are explicit about the aim to create a more balanced gender relationship.

Tempts users to guess
The CVA Framework offers a temptation to people with a relatively superficial knowledge of the situation to make guesses.

Not a participatory tool
Practitioners report that the framework does not lend itself to participatory uses; they have found its concepts difficult to use directly with communities experiencing crisis.

Assumes planners have a neutral agenda regarding gender relations
The model assumes that planners and implementing agencies are neutral agents. It is important to carry out an institutional analysis of implementing organisations in order to highlight opportunities and constraints within them regarding gender-aware planning and implementation.

Adaptation

Categories of capacities and vulnerabilities have been expanded to include those which relate to the human body and control over it, and one's sexuality.

Further reading

The framework is outlined in a user-friendly manner in Anderson M, Woodrow P, *Rising from the Ashes: Development Strategies in Times of Disaster*, Westview Press, Boulder and San Francisco, and UNESCO, Paris 1989. Second edition by Lynne Rienner Publishers, Inc., 1998. The first part of the book presents the framework, the lessons learned, and guidelines. The second part presents 11 case studies, none of which have a strong gender perspective.

2.6 | Women's Empowerment (Longwe) Framework

Background

The Women's Empowerment (Longwe) Framework was developed by Sara Hlupekile Longwe, a consultant on gender and development based in Lusaka, Zambia.

Aims of the framework

The Longwe framework is intended to help planners question what women's empowerment and equality means in practice, and, from this point, to assess critically to what extent a development intervention is supporting this empowerment. Longwe defines women's empowerment as enabling women to take an equal place with men, and to participate equally in the development process in order to achieve control over the factors of production on an equal basis with men.

The framework

Sara Longwe argues that much of the development literature examines to what extent equality between women and men has been achieved according to the conventional sectors of economy and society: equality in education, employment, and so on. This system of analysing equality by sectors concentrates on separate areas of social life, rather than on women's equality in the development process. In the Longwe framework, development means enabling people to take charge of their own lives, and escape from poverty; poverty is seen as arising not from lack of productivity, but from oppression and exploitation.

Longwe's framework is based on the notion of five different 'levels of equality'. The extent to which these are present in any area of social or economic life determines the level of women's empowerment. The Longwe Framework also enables gender and development workers to analyse development organisations' degree of commitment to women's equality and empowerment. They do this first by identifying which 'levels of equality' are addressed by a particular intervention, and second by assessing which 'levels of recognition' of women's issues exist in the project objectives. It is also possible to produce a profile of an entire development programme, categorising its projects in terms of the levels of equality which they address, and their level of recognition of women's issues. This might be part of an exercise undertaken by a large development organisation which wishes to assess its entire country programme from a gender perspective. Such an exercise is partially illustrated in case study 2 below.

The Longwe Framework is discussed in 'Gender awareness: the missing element in the Third World development project' by Sara Hlupekile Longwe in *Changing Perceptions: writings on gender and development,* edited by Tina Wallace with Candida March, Oxfam, 1991. It also appears in the form of training materials in the *Oxfam Gender Training Manual* edited by Suzanne Williams, Oxfam, 1994. The information on the framework in this section is adapted from both these sources.

Women's Empowerment Tool 1: Levels of equality

The Longwe Framework centres on the concept of five 'levels of equality', which indicate the extent to which women are equal with men, and have achieved empowerment. The levels of equality can be used to assess the likelihood of particular development interventions promoting equality and women's empowerment.

The levels of equality are:

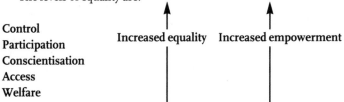

Control
Participation
Conscientisation
Access
Welfare

These levels of equality are hierarchical. If a development intervention focuses on the higher levels, there is a greater likelihood that women's empowerment will be increased by the intervention than if the project focuses on the lower levels. If the intervention concentrates only on welfare, it is very unlikely that women will find the project empowering. Equal participation in the decision-making process about certain resources is more important for achieving women's empowerment than equal access to resources; and neither participation nor access are as important as equal control.

When the levels of equality are used to analyse the impact of development interventions on women's equality and empowerment, it is important to understand that an ideal intervention does not necessarily show activities on every level. In fact, an intervention which is empowering for women will have many components which fit into the higher categories, but none in the lower ones. The 'Welfare' level restricts its focus to access to material resources. Therefore, an intervention which addressed control of resources would be classified at a higher level – under 'Control'. It would be seen as concerned with a higher degree of women's equality and empowerment.

Longwe's levels of equality are defined in more detail as follows:

Welfare: Longwe defines this as the level of women's material welfare, relative to men. Do women have equal access to resources such as food supply, income and, medical care?

Access: This is defined as women's access to the factors of production on an equal basis with men; equal access to land, labour, credit, training, marketing facilities, and all public services and benefits. Longwe points out that equality of access is obtained by applying the principle of equality of opportunity, which typically entails the reform of the law and administrative practice to remove all forms of discrimination against women.

Conscientisation: This is understood in the Longwe Framework as a conscious understanding of the difference between sex and gender, and an awareness that gender roles are cultural and can be changed. 'Conscientisation' also involves a belief that the sexual division of labour should be fair and agreeable to both sides, and not involve the economic or political domination of one sex by the other. A belief in sexual equality is the basis of gender awareness, and of collective participation in the process of women's development.

Participation: Longwe defines this as women's equal participation in the decision-making process, in policy-making, planning, and administration. It is a particularly important aspect of development projects, where participation means involvement in needs-assessment, project formulation, implementation, and evaluation. Equality of participation means involving women in making the decisions by which their community will be affected, in a proportion which matches their proportion in the wider community.

Control: This term denotes women's control over the decision-making process through conscientisation and mobilisation, to achieve equality of control over the factors of production and the distribution of benefits. Equality of control means a balance of control between men and women, so that neither side dominates.

Women's Empowerment Tool 2: Level of recognition of 'women's issues'

Longwe asserts that it is not only important to assess the levels of women's empowerment which a development intervention seeks to address. It is also important to identify the extent to which the project objectives are concerned with women's development, to establish whether women's issues are ignored or recognised. Longwe uses a very specific definition of 'women's issues', meaning all issues concerned with women's equality in any social or economic role, and involving any of the levels of equality (welfare, access, conscientisation, participation, control). In other words, an issue becomes a 'women's issue' when it looks at the relationship between men and women, rather than simply at women's traditional and subordinate sex-stereotyped gender roles.

The Longwe Framework does not specify whether development interventions should target women-only, men-only, or mixed groups. Women's empowerment must be the concern of both women and men, and the degree to which the project is defined as potentially empowering women is defined by the extent to which it addresses women's issues.

Longwe identifies three different levels of recognition of women's issues in project design:

Negative level: At this level, the project objectives make no mention of women's issues. Experience has shown that women are very likely to be left worse off by such a project.

Neutral level: This is also known as the conservative level. Project objectives recognise women's issues, but concerns remain that the project intervention does not leave women worse off than before.

Positive level: At this level, the project objectives are positively concerned with women's issues, and with improving the position of women relative to men.

Example of Women's Empowerment Framework Tools 1 and 2

Project title: _____

Level of recognition \ Levels of equality	Negative	Neutral	Positive
Control			
Participation			
Conscientisation			
Access			
Welfare			

Case study: A fishing community in Chile

Project background

The project examined in this case study is based in a sea port in Chile of about 130,000 people.[9] Fishing has always been the mainstay of the town's and the region's economy. Men used to catch and dive for seafood, while women's tasks included selling the fish and mending the nets. Now, fishing is mainly controlled by multinational corporations (MNCs) with huge shipping vessels and factory ships, and fish stocks are being culled at unsustainable rates. Although trade union activity used to be relatively high in the region, the fact that MNCs only tend to employ people unaffiliated to a union has caused the numbers to drop radically.

There are few independent fishermen or fishsellers left, resulting in rising unemployment among men and an associated rise in alcoholism. Women tends to work in the local factories, under very poor conditions and at poor rates of pay, or in domestic service.

The project has a number of programmes, one of which is the Woman's Programme; it aims to mobilise women and support their self-empowerment. At first, its main activities were education on issues such as health, rights, organisation, and leadership. After some time, the women asked the project to begin supporting productive activities. The project now supports women's groups working in low-cost greenhouses and handicrafts, among other such activities. Here, the Woman's Programme is examined using Longwe's Women's Empowerment Framework.

Using Women's Empowerment Tool 1: Levels of equality

Applying Longwe's levels of equality, it becomes clear that the emphasis of the programme is at the conscientisation and participation levels: increasing women's self-confidence, and their capacity to participate in decision-making processes, through education. Below, examples are given of how the project might further be examined in terms of the levels.

Welfare

The project has no activities simply directed at increasing women's access to material resources relative to men. In Longwe's terminology, all levels of the Women's Programme are concerned with higher levels of equality, since all the activities start from the premise of trying to increase women's levels of confidence, awareness, and control.

Access

As described above, the project has now started to support women in their wish to be involved in productive activities. From May to August, it is not possible to grow vegetables in the area, so they are brought from the centre of Chile at great cost. The project held a workshop for one group to discuss the idea of growing vegetables in low-cost greenhouses made out of plastic sheeting. Now, a number of groups run such greenhouses. The women contribute the wood and labour for the construction and then take turns looking after the vegetables. Here, the project can be seen to be working at the 'Access' level of equality, since it is increasing women's access to the factors of production (in this case communal land, greenhouses, and vegetables).

The project also saw equal wages as a key issue for women: this also comes under the level of 'Access', since it is access to equal income. However, the project's attempt to organise women working in the factories into a coherent movement failed. Women working the long shifts did not have time to attend meetings and they were afraid of being sacked if their organising activities were discovered.

Conscientisation

Raising Awareness about gender issues forms a large part of the Chilean Women's Programme. According to the development workers, their most important objective is 'to provide women with general education, increase their self-confidence and awareness, and make them realise that they are important'. The project starts its work with local women with self-confidence workshops, using discussion groups, role-plays, and games on such issues as 'how do I consider my role in the family and community?' They then move on to mini-workshops on health, the rights and responsibilities of women, women's work and labour rights, human rights and the national situation, the history of the women's movement and the trade union movement in Chile, and forms of organisation.

The project has also tried to raise gender issues with men. For instance, they printed leaflets on violence against women and distributed them to men in the streets on a national day of action about the issue.

Participation

Central to the project's approach is the idea that project activities must not impose ideas on people - in this case, local women must diagnose what they want and need. Through the activities and dialogue mentioned in the previous section on conscientisation, the objectives of the programmes evolved.

The project has given attention to increasing women's participation in decision-making processes. At first women were reluctant to take up special positions within each of the groups. Consequently, two to three local women from each of the project groups now attend a leadership-training programme, which aims to help them feel confident in running the groups. On a bigger scale, the project also persuaded two local women to stand in local council elections - unfortunately they did not win.

Control

Women are in control of the production and benefits from the vegetables in the greenhouses, both for consumption and for selling at a profit. The project also teaches account-keeping and administration, because otherwise the women would need to rely on someone else to keep the accounts, lessening the women's level of control over profits and resources.

The above findings can be represented in a table, disaggregated into the two main areas of production in the greenhouses, and political participation (see overleaf).

Using Women's Empowerment Tool 1: Levels of equality

	Greenhouses	Political participation
Welfare	No	No
Access	Yes	No
Conscientisation	No	Yes
Participation	Yes	Yes
Control	Yes	No

Using Women's Empowerment Tool 2 – Level of recognition of women's issues

The Chile project would be classified as having a positive level, because the project's implementers have a high level of recognition of women's issues.

Using the Longwe Framework to analyse a multiple-project development programme

To demonstrate the use of the Longwe Framework in analysing an entire development programme, an imaginary programme with three sectors

Using Women's Empowerment Framework Tools 1 and 2

Sector	Project	Level of Equality					Level of recognition of women's issues
		Welfare	Access	Conscien- tisation	Partici- pation	Control	
Agriculture							
Education & training	Political participation	No	No	Yes	Yes	No	Positive
Commerce & industry	Greenhouse	No	Yes	No	Yes	Yes	Positive

(agriculture, education and training, and commerce and industry) has been created in the table above. This imaginary programme includes the findings from the Chilean case study referred to above. Other projects would need to be similarly assessed, and added to the profile of the programme.

Commentary

Uses

For transformatory planning, monitoring, and evaluation
The Longwe Framework can be a useful framework for planning, monitoring and evaluation, allowing users to question whether their interventions have transformatory potential. It can be a useful tool to strengthen the translation of a commitment to women's empowerment into actual plans and policy.

For training on technical and transformatory issues
In training the Longwe Framework is taught as part of work on planning and evaluation. It is also useful as a way of encouraging an examination of what is meant by empowerment.

Why it appeals

Moves beyond the concept of practical and strategic gender needs to show them as a progression
The Longwe Framework has much in common with the Moser Framework's concept of practical and strategic gender needs. However, it moves away from this restrictive distinction, which Longwe views as unhelpful. The Longwe Framework shows that development interventions as containing both 'practical' and 'strategic' elements. The progression from practical to strategic depends on the extent to which the intervention has potential to 'empower'.

Emphasises empowerment
The method Longwe uses is particularly useful in explaining why 'empowerment' is intrinsic to the process of development. It therefore illuminates aspects of development work which had previously not been sufficiently recognised or appreciated.

Strongly ideological
The framework has a very strong political perspective. It emphasises that development means overcoming women's inequality compared to men in every respect.

Useful to identify the gap between rhetoric and reality in interventions
For groups committed to equality and empowerment, whose projects may not yet reflect this commitment, the Longwe Framework is a particularly valuable method of analysis. It permits an assessment of where women already have equality, and what still remains to be done.

Potential limitations

Not a 'complete' framework

The Longwe Framework is perhaps best seen as part of a 'tool kit', rather than as a stand-alone framework, for the following reasons.

- It is static and takes no account of how situations change over time;
- It looks at the relationship between men and women only in terms of equality – rather than at the complicated system of rights, claims, and responsibilities which exists between them;
- It does not consider other forms of inequality, and can encourage a misleading view of women as a homogeneous group;
- It does not examine the institutions and organisations involved;
- It does not examine the macro-environment;
- It deals in very broad generalities only.

Hierarchy of levels may make users think that empowerment is a linear process

Users may assume that in order to reach the level of 'Control', an intervention will have had to meet all the previous four levels. As explained above, this is not the case. An empowering intervention is likely to include resource considerations at the level of 'Control', but not at the levels of 'Welfare' and 'Access'.

Hierarchy of levels does not allow for relative importance of different resources

The hierarchy can fall apart when one tries to consider the importance of different resources. A strict interpretation of the value of levels might lead to the conclusion that control (for example, of hoes) contributes more to women's development than access (for example, to land).

Hierarchy of levels does not help to differentiate between marginally different impacts

Defining development only in terms of women's empowerment can tempt users to focus only on women rather than on gender relations

The emphasis on women's empowerment is one of the strengths of this framework. However, it is also one of its weaknesses, since it can encourage analysis of women without an understanding of how women and men relate (including how they are connected), and without an understanding of men's needs and interests.

Strongly ideological

This framework can be too confrontational to be used with those who are not committed to women's empowerment.

Further reading

As stated earlier, this framework is discussed in both Williams S (1994) *Oxfam Gender Training Manual*, Oxfam (UK and Ireland), Oxford, and Wallace T and March C (1991) *Changing Perceptions: Writings on Gender and Development*, Oxfam (UK and Ireland), Oxford.

2.7 | Social Relations Approach

Background

The Social Relations Approach to gender and development planning has been developed by Naila Kabeer at the Institute of Development Studies, Sussex University, UK, in collaboration with policy-makers, academics, and activists, primarily from the South. It has been used by government departments and NGOs for planning programmes in a number of countries. The thinking has a socialist feminist background.

Key elements of the approach are:

- the goal of development as human well-being;

- the concept of social relations;

- institutional analysis.

The following discussion of the Social Relations Approach adapts work by Naila Kabeer in *Reversed Realities: Gender Hierarchies in Development Thought*, Verso, UK, 1994. It also draws on an internal paper written for Oxfam by Naila Kabeer and Ramya Subrahmanian in 1996, entitled 'Institutions, relations and outcomes: concepts and methods for training in gender-aware planning'.

Aims of the framework

The Social Relations Approach is intended as a method of analysing existing gender inequalities in the distribution of resources, responsibilities, and power, and for designing policies and programmes which enable women to be agents of their own development. The framework uses concepts rather than tools to concentrate on the relationships between people and their relationship to resources and activities – and how these are re-worked through 'institutions' such as the state or the market.

Kabeer states that a narrow application of the Social Relations Approach, examining a particular institution, will highlight how gender inequality is formed and reproduced in individual institutions. A broader application, focusing on a number of institutions in a given context, will reveal how gender and other inequalities cross-cut each other through different institutions' interaction, thus producing situations of specific disadvantage for individuals.

The framework

The main concepts of the Social Relations Approach are:

Social Relations Approach Concept 1: Development as increasing human well-being

In the Social Relations Approach, development is primarily about increasing human well-being. It is not simply about economic growth or improved productivity. Human well-being is seen as concerning survival, security, and autonomy, where autonomy means the ability to participate fully in those decisions that shape one's choices and one's life chances, at both the personal and the collective level. Therefore, development interventions must be assessed not only in terms of technical efficiency, but also in terms of how well they contribute to the broader goals of survival, security, and human dignity.

Importantly, it follows from this that the concept of production does not just include market production but all the activities which contribute to human well-being – including all those tasks which people perform to reproduce human labour (caring, nurturing, looking after the sick), those which poor people carry out to survive; and those which people perform in caring for their environment which ultimately assures their livelihoods.

Social Relations Approach Concept 2: Social relations

Kabeer uses the term 'social relations' to describe the structural relationships that create and reproduce systemic differences in the positioning of different groups of people. Such relationships determine who we are, what our roles and responsibilities are, and what claims we can make; they determine our rights, and the control that we have over our own lives and those of others. Social relations produce cross-cutting inequalities, which ascribe each individual a position in the structure and hierarchy of their society. Gender relations are one type of social relations (sometimes known as the social relations of gender). Others include those of class, race, ethnicity, and so on.

Social relations change; they are not fixed or immutable. Changes at the macro level can bring about change in social relations. Human action can also do so, as is evident in the overturning of apartheid in South Africa, and the consequent changes in that country's social relations of race.

Social relations also determine what tangible and intangible resources are available to groups and individuals. Poverty arises out of people's unequal social relations, which dictate unequal relations to resources, claims, and responsibilities. (Simply put, people don't start at the same point in the social system, and as a consequence have very different capacities to take advantage of change or the status quo.) Poor people in general, and poor women in particular, are often excluded from formal allocations of resources, so they draw on other resources – determined by their social relations – which play a critical part in their survival strategies. For example, poor women often rely on networks of family and friends to manage their workload. Resources of this kind, available through social relations, can be so important that some would say that 'poverty is being alone'.

Often, poor people have access to resources mainly through social relationships based on patronage and dependency, where they have to trade in their autonomy in return for security. Development must also look at supporting relationships which build on solidarity and reciprocity, and which build autonomy, rather than reduce it.

Social Relations Approach Concept 3: Institutional analysis

The underlying causes of gender inequality are not confined to the household and family but are reproduced across a range of institutions, including the international community, the state, and the market place.

Definitions of 'institution' and 'organisation'

Kabeer defines an institution as a framework of rules for achieving certain social or economic goals. Institutions ensure the production, reinforcement, and reproduction of social relations and thereby create and perpetuate social difference and social inequality. Organisations, on the other hand, are defined as the specific structural forms that institutions take (North 1990, quoted in Kabeer 1994). Gender-awareness requires us to analyse how these institutions actually create and reproduce inequalities.

Four key institutional locations

Kabeer suggests that, for analytical purposes, it is useful to think of four key institutional realms – the state, the market, the community, and family/

Example of Social Relations Concept 3: Institutional analysis	
Key institutional locations	**Organisational/structural form**
State	Legal, military, administrative organisations
Market	Firms, financial corporations, farming enterprises, multinationals, and so on
Community	Village tribunals, voluntary associations, informal networks, patron-client relationships, NGOs
Family/kinship	Household, extended families, lineage groupings, and so on

kinship. One could choose to add the international community. To give an example of how an institution relates to organisations, the state provides the larger institutional framework for a range of legal, military, and administrative organisations. Other examples are listed in the table above.

Challenging the ideological neutrality and independence of institutions

The Social Relations Approach challenges two myths about institutions on which much prevailing planning is based: that they are ideologically neutral, and that they are separate entities and that therefore a change to one of them will not affect the others.

Challenging the myth of ideological neutrality, Kabeer argues that institutions produce, reinforce, and reproduce social difference and inequalities. Few institutions admit to ideologies of gender or any other form of inequality. Instead, each institution has an 'official' ideology which accompanies all its policy and planning. The 'official' ideologies which tend to dominate planning practice are based on the following assumptions.

- the state pursues the national interest and national welfare;

- the market pursues about profit maximisation;

- the community, including NGOs, is about service provision;

- family/kinship is about altruism; it is a co-operative, not a conflictual, institution.

Kabeer argues that, in order to understand how social difference and inequalities (in roles, responsibilities, claims, and power) are produced, reinforced, and reproduced through institutions, we must move beyond the official ideology of bureaucratic neutrality, and scrutinise the actual rules and practices of institutions to uncover their core values and assumptions.

The Social Relations Approach also challenges the myth of the independence, or separateness, of institutions. It asserts that they are inter-related, and that a change in the policy or practice in one institution will cause changes in the others. For instance, it is often assumed in development work that a change in one sphere – for example, an intervention which provides inputs to enable men in the community to grow more cash crops – will be self-contained, and will not have an impact on the other spheres, such as the household. However, we all know that this official picture hides much. Changes in policy or practice on the part of the state and market affect relationships within the family, and changes within the family also have an impact on the market and the state (see diagram on p 108).

Development planners and practitioners must therefore pay attention to the interactions between institutions. In planning an intervention which will deals with institutions such as the household or the community , an NGO will first need to know what the state's policies are, and who is setting the agenda for the country where it aims to work. They must also recognise that institutions are capable of change – indeed, they adapt constantly, in order to respond to change in the external context. Institutional change is brought about through the practices of different institutional actors, and through processes of bargaining and negotiation.

Five aspects of social relations shared by institutions

Kabeer states that institutions differ in many ways; for example, they vary in different cultures. However, she emphasises that they do have some common aspects. The Social Relations Approach states that all institutions possess five distinct, but inter-related, dimensions of social relationships: rules, resources, people, activities, and power. These dimensions are significant to the analysis of social inequality in general, and gender inequality in particular. Examining institutions on the basis of their rules, practices, people, distribution of resources, and their authority and control structures, helps you understand who does what, who gains, who loses (which men and which women). This is called undertaking an institutional analysis.

1. Rules: how things get done

Institutional behaviour is governed by rules. These may be official and written down. They may be unofficial and expressed through norms, values, laws, traditions, and customs. What rules do is to allow or constrain the following:

- what is done;

- how it is done;

- by whom it will be done;

- who will benefit.

Rules allow everyday decisions to be made with the minimum of effort. Their disadvantage is that they entrench ways of doing things, often to such an extent that they seem natural or unchangeable.

2. Activities: what is done?

Institutions do things; they try to achieve goals by following their own rules. These activities can be productive, distributive, or regulative. It is important to ask the following questions about activities:

- who does what?

- who gets what?

- who can claim what?

Institutions' rules ensure that there is a routinised pattern of practice for carrying out tasks. As a consequence, certain tasks get attached to certain social groups, so that it seems that these groups are only capable of doing that particular task. For example, the strong association of women with the tasks of caring for the young, the sick, and the elderly – both within the household and within state and market institutions – is often explained in terms of their 'natural' maternal predispositions.

Rewards are attached to tasks; these vary according to who does what. For instance, doing the housework receives less recognition than ploughing the family land. Such a hierarchy of rewards reinforces inequalities between women and men, or between age groups.

People who only carry out a particular task become very good at it. In this sense, the gender division of labour has the effect of a self-fulfilling prophesy. The attributes which give women an advantage in certain jobs and occupations – nurturing skills, patience, managing budgets – have been acquired through their cultural assignment to women of the tasks and responsibilities within which these traits are likely to be developed.

In the final analysis, institutional practice must be changed if unequal relations are to be transformed.

3. Resources: what is used, what is produced?

Institutions also mobilise and distribute resources. These may be human resources (for example, labour, education, and skills), material ones (food, assets, land, or money), or intangible ones (information, political, clout, goodwill, or contacts).

Very often, the distribution of resources corresponds to an institution's rules. Thus, in societies where women are required to contribute to family food provisions, they are more likely to enjoy independent access to land and other resources. By contrast, in societies where it is men's responsibility to feed the family, men are given privileged access to resources within the household, but also within state and market institutions.

4. People: who is in, who is out, who does what?

Institutions deal with people and are selective about:

- who they allow in and whom they exclude;

- who is assigned various resources, tasks, and responsibilities;

- who is positioned where in the hierarchy.

This selection reflects class, gender, and other social inequalities. For example, if you look at the household you will find that specific households allow specific people in – perhaps one is not meant to marry across class, race, or ethnic dividing lines. The market also excludes and includes specific categories of people. In Britain, high-powered jobs are normally held by white, English, middle- or upper-class men.

5. *Power: who decides, and whose interests are served?*

Institutions embody relations of authority and control. Few institutions are egalitarian, even if they profess to be so. The unequal distribution of resources and responsibilities, together with the official and unofficial rules which promote and legitimise this distribution, ensures that some institutional actors have authority and control over others. These individuals then promote practices which entrench their privileged position, and they are most likely to resist change.

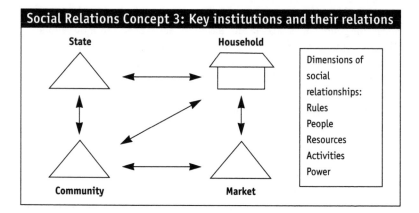

Social Relations Concept 3: Key institutions and their relations

State   Household

Community   Market

Dimensions of social relationships:
Rules
People
Resources
Activities
Power

Social Relations Approach Concept 4: Institutional gender policies

Naila Kabeer classifies policies into three types, depending on the degree to which they recognise and address gender issues (see diagram next page).

Gender-blind policies: These recognise no distinction between the sexes. Policies incorporate biases in favour of existing gender relations and therefore tend to exclude women.

Gender-aware policies: These recognise that women as well as men are development actors, and that they are constrained in different, often unequal, ways as potential participants and beneficiaries in the development process. They may consequently have differing and sometimes conflicting needs, interests, and priorities. Gender-aware policies can be further sub-divided into three policy types.

Gender-neutral policy approaches use the knowledge of gender differences in a given society to overcome biases in development interventions. They aim to ensure that interventions target and benefit both sexes effectively to meet their practical gender needs. Gender-neutral policies work within the existing gender division of resources and responsibilities.

Gender-specific policies use the knowledge of gender differences in a given context to respond to the practical gender needs of either women or men; they also work within the existing gender division of resources and responsibilities.

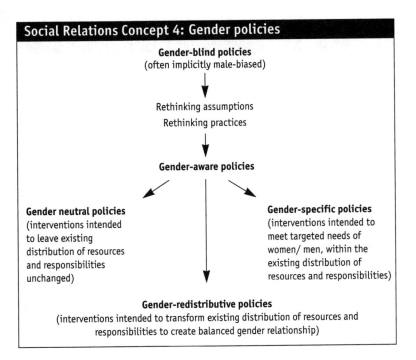

Social Relations Concept 4: Gender policies

Gender-blind policies
(often implicitly male-biased)

Rethinking assumptions
Rethinking practices

Gender-aware policies

Gender neutral policies
(interventions intended to leave existing distribution of resources and responsibilities unchanged)

Gender-specific policies
(interventions intended to meet targeted needs of women/ men, within the existing distribution of resources and responsibilities)

Gender-redistributive policies
(interventions intended to transform existing distribution of resources and responsibilities to create balanced gender relationship)

Gender-redistributive policies are interventions which intend to transform existing distributions to create a more balanced relationship between women and men. They may target both women and men, or only one group specifically. Gender-redistributive policies touch on strategic gender interests; they may work on women's practical gender needs, but do so in ways which have transformatory potential, i.e. which help create supportive conditions for women to empower themselves.

These different approaches are not mutually exclusive, and one may be a precursor to another. For instance, in situations were gender-blind planning has been the norm, moving towards gender-neutral policies would be a significant shift forward. In some situations, it may be counter-productive to start with gender-redistributive policies, and a better approach may be a gender-specific policy, meeting practical needs.

Social Relations Approach Concept 5: Immediate, underlying and structural causes

In analysing a situation in order to plan an intervention, this framework explores the immediate, underlying, and structural factors which cause the problems, and their effects on the various actors involved. The analysis can be presented in a table (see table overleaf for an example), or as a written report (see case study 2 for an example), as you prefer.

Example of Social Relations Concept 5: Causes and effects	
Long-term effects	
Intermediate effects	
Immediate effects	
The core problem	
Immediate causes at • household level • community level • market level • state level	
Intermediate causes at • household level • community level • market level • state level	
Structural causes at • household level • community level • market level • state level	

Case studies of the Social Relations Approach

Case study 1: Poor people's access to credit in India – institutional analysis and design of development intervention

This case study is adapted from a 1996 paper by Naila Kabeer and Ramya Subrahmanian, of the Institute for Development Studies (IDS), University of Sussex. They analysed the problems of the poor in relation to credit in India, looking both at general and at gender-specific constraints which hamper poor men's and women's access to formal credit institutions. This analysis was used to spell out the consequences of this exclusion for their survival and well-being. Kabeer and Subrahmanian first carried out an institutional analysis of the causes and effects of reduced access to credit, using Concepts 3 and 5 of the Social Relations Approach. The findings are shown in the table on p 111.

In order to then plan an appropriate intervention, they chose a commonly used evaluation tool, the Logical Framework[10] (see pp 112-114). This tool helps you decide how an intervention can effectively address the issues uncovered in the institutional analysis. It makes you consider what you want to achieve, how you will do it, and how you will know whether you have achieved it.

Using Social Relations Concept 6: Causes and effects analysis	
Long-term effects	• Indebtedness; vulnerability; impoverishment; disempowerment; • Women's disempowerment vis-à-vis men; gender inequalities in physical well-being;
Intermediate effects	• Shortfalls in consumption; reduced capacity to recover from crisis; • Gender inequalities in distribution of consumption shortfalls; increased dependence on male income;
Immediate effects	• Fluctuations in household income flows; resort to unreliable or exploitative forms of credit; • Access to credit depends on sexual exploitation;
The core problem	• Lack of access to formal-sector credit; • Gender inequalities in gaining access to formal-sector credit;
Immediate causes • Household level	• Lack of collateral**; lack of self-confidence; uncertain repayment capacity; • Intensified gender disadvantage for women regarding collateral, self-confidence, and repayment capacity; • Constraints on women's social and physical mobility;
• Bank level	• Collateral requirements; complex and inflexible procedures; perceptions of poor people as high-risk borrowers; • Discriminatory official and unofficial barriers against women; economic invisibility of women's enterprise;
Intermediate causes • Household level	• Low-productivity enterprises; uncertainty of returns; illiteracy; ignorance about banking procedures; class distance from bank personnel; survival imperatives; • Intensified gender disadvantage for women in all the aspects listed above; greater emphasis on survival in women's enterprises; • Social isolation; physical distancing of women from bank personnel; uncertain control over loans or the proceeds from loans;
• Bank level	• Risk-averse culture; perceived costs of lending to the poor; class distance from the poor; • Ideological norms about female dependency; greater perceived costs of lending to women; physical distancing from women borrowers;
Structural causes • Bank level • Household level	• Entrenched banking practices; unequal distribution of assets; imperfect financial markets; inadequate educational provision; • Ideology of male breadwinner; gender-segmented labour markets; gender-biased institutional practices; gender inequalities in intra-household power relations.

Case study 1: Designing a development intervention

Objectives	Activities	Indicators
Long-term objective		
Ensuring regularised access to institutional credit for women and men from low-income households	Meetings with bank officials by groups' representatives	Number of meetings; composition of group representation at meetings; group preparation and outcome of meetings
	Agreement of bank procedures for lending to group-guaranteed members	Extent and nature of participation in designing bank procedures; gender-awareness of new bank procedures
	Phasing out of agency support for groups	Institutional capacity of groups (for example, management skills, democratic leadership structures, equity in participation at all levels, financial viability, and sustainability)
	Expansion into wider range of enterprises by both men and women	Gender-disaggregated data on nature, viability and success of enterprises; women's participation in non-traditional activities
Intermediate objective		
Promotion of women's and men's credit-management groups to invest their self-generated capital funds productively	Training members of older groups in leadership skills and more advanced forms of financial management • in enterprise development and management • women-only groups in non-traditional skills and enterprises	Gender-disaggregated data on participation in training; impact of training on women's and men's financial skills, awareness, confidence, and management skills; impact on productivity; women acquiring new, non-traditional skills; wider range of enterprises undertaken by women;
	Dissemination of knowledge about bank procedures	Outreach of information; gender-aware literature on banking procedures; use of *continued...*

Objectives	Activities	Indicators
		different media; access of illiterate and neo-literate women and men to information
	Developing group-based approaches to overcome mobility constraints	Increased participation in distant markets; increased access to and use of means of transport; direct interactions between group representatives and financial institutions
	Building access to other technical departments of government	Meetings between government departments and groups; successful resolution of group demands
Immediate objective Formation of separate self-help groups of poor women and men to promote saving and lending for self-identified needs	Recruitment of male and female staff and fieldworkers	Numbers of men and women at all levels of the organisation; egalitarian/ transformatory gender division of labour within organisation
	Training of staff and fieldworkers in group-information skills, gender-awareness, and financial management	Numbers of training programmes conducted, extent of follow-up; participation of male and female staff; attention to gender content in training programmes; changes in practice as a result of training
	Construction of group's centre close to target groups	Number of centres; group members' satisfaction with location of centres; increase in women members' participation in group activities
	Adoption of sensitive and flexible rules of group saving and lending	Consultation with poorer members in developing rules; group members' satisfaction with rules; increase in participation

continued...

Objectives	Activities	Indicators
Immediate objectives		by poorer members, particularly women, in group saving and lending; reduced dependence on or better terms from money lenders
	Training of group members in basic accounting skills	Numbers of women and men trained, application of accounting skills by members to relevant activities
	Use of literacy and numeracy for 'conscienti-sation' around class and gender issues for male and female groups	Use of examples with transformatory potential in training material full participation by women and men in the training; changed perceptions and practices attributable to the training
	Building group responsibility for loan recovery	Adoption of processes/ rules within group to manage default; improve-ment in repayment rates

Case study 2: Issues facing disabled women in Lebanon – external institutional analysis

The following case study (written by Lina Abu Habib, Project Officer in Oxfam's Lebanon Programme, in June 1995) illustrates how Concept 3 of the Social Relations Approach was used for planning purposes by Oxfam, to achieve a wide-ranging analysis of gender and disability in Lebanon. Institutional Analysis was carried out on both the external context and the internal context in which Oxfam worked. However, what follows here is a shortened version of the external analysis only.

After a brief description of attitudes to disability before Lebanon's civil war (which lasted from 1975-90), each of the four institutions in Concept 3 of the Social Relations Approach (state, market, community, and household) is analysed, outlining the situation before, during, and after the civil war.

Background: external environment before the war

Disability was considered an affliction which must be borne by the disabled person and his or her family. Disabled persons were almost totally marginalised from the public sphere. The state did not provide any significant services, education, or employment. No organisations or unions of disabled persons existed. Work with the disabled took place entirely within charitable and religious institutions. No consideration was given to the special needs of disabled women or women carers.

State

The war years

The state assumed some responsibility for the war-disabled as their number increased visibly. The state had very conservative attitudes on disabled persons' integration and independence. The deteriorating economic situation led to a further decrease in the resources available for the disabled. No specific attention was paid to disabled women.

The post-war period

As part of the general post-war reconstruction, rehabilitation, and modernisation effort, some laws were reviewed, albeit very slowly. The National Council for Disabled's Affairs was created, which officially recognises the representation of disabled persons. At the level of public discourse, there was a declared interest in disability issues. Some government bodies proved to be open to issues of disability, and sympathetic to new interventions. Some politicians came to hold progressive, avant-garde views on disability. But issues perceived to be related to the arena of social affairs still remained low on the state's priority list.

Market

Before and throughout the war

Local labour laws and the labour market as a whole discriminated against disabled persons. Both the public and the private sector were ill equipped to employ or even accommodate people with disabilities. The economic crisis, which escalated from 1986 onward, has further undermined disabled persons' access to the employment market.

The post-war period

The state took small, localised, but decisive, steps towards the integration and absorption of persons with disabilities into the public-service sector. However, many persons with disabilities (particularly women and poor persons who lack particular skills) remain excluded. Lobbying continues to change some discriminatory laws (labour law, social security, and so on). There are occasional nation-wide media campaigns which emphasise that disabled persons are able, and have the right, to assume gainful employment. Moreover, some efforts are made to promote access to employment through training, credit schemes, and so on.

Community/ NGOs

The war years

Emergency relief and service provision were considered priorities for NGOs. People with disabilities organised in groups and managed to gain access to international funding agencies. Different NGOs were created, many with a large constituency base. NGOs have succeeded in raising the profile of disability: for example, the national media have become more concerned. NGOs themselves have become aware that they need to develop lobbying and advocacy skills.

The post-war period

Some degree of grassroots mobilisation has been achieved. NGOs have an increased ability to network locally and regionally. They have developed and maintained links with key actors, decision makers, and some national fora. There have been some successes in lobbying and advocacy – disability is now on the official agenda. NGOs have expanded in size and in their scope of programmes, although foreign funding is generally decreasing. NGOs place more emphasis on collection and use of empirical data.

Big charitable institutions are still powerful and feel threatened by disabled persons' NGOs. However, these have difficulties in working together and in developing much needed professional competencies. They are still weak in their planning and organisation, and there are obvious problems related to leadership. Leadership positions are mainly assumed by disabled men.

The gender perspective within NGOs remains weak or tokenistic; indeed, it is sometimes absent. Active disabled women are now seeking more attention and consideration for the specific needs and situation of disabled women. The reduced life chances for disabled people are worse in rural areas, where there is almost no state intervention or NGO activity.

Household

The household is the main location of care for people with disabilities. Women are usually the main carers in the household, and they are least likely to be provided with support and/ or compensation. Women are also least likely to be the decision-makers in the household. Discrimination in access to resources often starts in the household: a disabled person's access to material and non-material resources largely depends on the main decision-maker's perception of his or her life chances.

Disability affects the reproductive role of women. It thus undermines their life chances considerably more than is the case for men with disabilities. A woman or girl with a disability is perceived to be unable to maintain a household and fulfil the roles of a 'proper' woman. Therefore, she is less likely to marry than disabled men; which increases her parent's financial burden. Women carers are often blamed for their children's disability.

Women with disabilities tend to be less mobile than men.

Commentary on Social Relations Approach

Uses

Useful for many purposes, and at many levels
The Social Relations Approach can be used for many purposes, including project planning and policy development. It can also be used at many levels, even at the international level.

Raises awareness of the importance of institutional analysis and can be used in training
The Social Relations Approach emphasises that institutional analysis is an important part of an organisational commitment to gender, and enables an organisation to translate an analysis into action.

Why it appeals

Gives a holistic analysis of poverty
The Social Relations Approach aims to give a fuller picture of poverty by recognising and highlighting the interacting and cross-cutting inequalities of class, gender, race, and so on. By doing so, the framework concentrates on structural analysis, material poverty, marginalisation, and powerlessness, and how those have evolved.

Aims to place gender at the centre of an entirely new framework for development theory and practice
The Social Relations Approach is an attempt to develop a new framework for development thinking – one where gender is central to the analysis. It is not an attempt to develop an add-on methodology for gender, or a separate method of analysis and planning which can only be used for projects focusing on women.

Concentrates on institutions
The Social Relations Approach offers a way of understanding how various institutions inter-relate. Therefore it gives an insight into the roots of powerlessness, poverty, and women's subordination; but it also shows that institutions can bring about change. This framework concentrates on institutional analysis and highlights that there is no such thing as a neutral planner. Organisations using this framework are obliged to examine their own institutional practices and culture, as part of any planning process.

Links analysis at all levels
Each level of analysis is seen as linked to the others. The Social Relations Approach makes clear that what goes on in the household can subvert (deliberately or not) the policies of the state and market. It also shows that policies and practice at the middle level of community/ organisations can influence these relationships.

Can be used in a dynamic analysis

Rather than giving a snapshot of gender roles at a particular point in time, without discussing the processes which have led to this, the Social Relations Approach can be used to highlight the processes of impoverishment and empowerment, as shown in the case study of Lebanon.

Highlights gender relations and emphasises women's and men's different interests and needs

The Social Relations Approach emphasises the connectedness of men and women through their social relationships, as well as the ways in which these affect them differently, as separate groups.

Potential limitations

Emphasises structure rather than agency

The analysis produced by using the Social Relations Approach tends to give an impression of monolithic institutions, where change will be difficult. While this is, in balance, probably true, it can lead to losing sight of the potential for people to bring about change.

Gender may become subsumed in a complex examination of cross-cutting inequalities, posing an obstacle for political action

This framework can be used to examine all the cross-cutting inequalities that create institutional marginalisation. As such, women can get subsumed in many individual categories of, say, class or sector. Where this is the case, gender issues become fragmented within other issues of class, ethnicity, religion, and so on.

Complexity may intimidate

The Social Relations Approach can seem complicated, detailed, and demanding. Of course it is, like the complex reality it is encouraging users to analyse. But concepts from the framework can be used in considerably simplified form.

Adaptation: The institutional analysis can be performed using three rather than five categories: rules, practices, and power (which is manifested through the rules and practices).

Difficult to use with communities in a participatory way

The theoretical grasp necessary to distinguish between complex concepts such as 'institution' and 'organisation' make the Social Relations Approach unsuitable to use in a participatory way at community level.

Complexity means very detailed knowledge of context is needed

The framework is difficult to use fully in situations where there is not very much information available.

In reality, institutions do not have definite boundaries

In real life, the institutions of state, market, community, and household cannot be so neatly defined – there is overlap between them. It is critical to understand that this neat distinction is merely a device to enable an analysis.

Difficulty in determining what is an institution

Some Oxfam staff have criticised the definition of the 'community' as an institution, arguing that it is not an institution in the same way as the state and the market. Others have raised the question of organisational forms which are not institutions; for example, some organisational forms of cultural or religious expression would more appropriately be defined as movements rather than institutions.

Adaptation: Institutional analysis has been used to good effect on institutions within the community, such as religious practices and laws.

Further reading

The Social Relations Approach is discussed in *Reversed Realities: Gender Hierarchies in Development Thought* by Naila Kabeer, Verso 1994.

The framework is also set out in a paper entitled 'Institutions, Relations and Outcomes: Framework and Tools for Gender-Aware Planning', Naila Kabeer and Ramya Subrahmanian, IDS Discussion Paper 357, Brighton, 1996. Another version of the paper is available from Oxfam's Gender and Learning Team on request.

Bibliography

Anderson MB and Woodrow PJ (1989) *Rising from the Ashes: Development Strategies in Times of Disaster*, Westview Press, UNESCO, Paris. Second edition by Lynne Rienner Publishers, Inc, 1998.

Full details and case studies of the Capabilities and Vulnerabilities Analysis method (CVA) used in dealing with emergencies. This method begins from a basis of gender awareness and is an extremely useful tool.

Anderson MB and the UNHCR Senior Coordinator for Refugee Women (1992) *A Framework for People-Oriented Planning in Refugee Situations*, UNHCR.

This is a practical planning tool for refugee workers, and draws on the concepts of the gender-analysis framework published in *Gender Roles in Development Projects*, Overholt et al (see separate entry). It introduces the three-step framework analysing the refugee profile and context, activities comparing what the refugees did before the emergency, and use and control of resources. The framework is also presented in a UNHCR handbook *People-Oriented Planning at Work* using POP to improve UNHCR programming, 1994. This is more of a how-to-do manual, taking the reader through sector by sector (water, sanitation, health) from emergencies to repatriation.

Buvinic, M 'Projects for Women in the Third World: Explaining their Misbehaviour', in *World Development*, Vol 14 No.5, 1986.

Provides an interesting exploration of how different agendas have informed projects for women, and how understanding these agendas explains the fact that outcomes may be very different from those anticipated by implementing organisations.

Canadian Council for International Co-operation (1991) *Two Halves Make a Whole: Balancing Gender Relations in Development*, Canadian Council for International Co-operation.

A very useful handbook of gender and development training, in five sections including a general discussion of gender and development, gender and development training, case studies, and evolution of theories and practice. The second part contains some material for training including activities adapted from Harvard and Moser methods and sample formats for workshops, while the third and fourth parts have some useful case study presentations of the integration of gender into institutional programmes. (Also includes a resources section.)

Kabeer N (1994) *Reversed Realities: Gender Hierarchies in Development Thought* Verso, London.

Kabeer N and Subrahmanian R (1996) 'Institutions, Relations and Outcomes: Framework and Tools for Gender-Aware Planning', IDS Discussion Paper 357, Brighton. Another version available from Gender and Learning Team, Oxfam, 274 Banbury Road, Oxford OX2 7DZ.

This paper helps place the Social Relations Approach in context. It is written using complex terminology, but is rich in analysis and examples.

Longwe, S (1995) 'Supporting Women's Development in the Third World: Distinguishing between Intervention and Interference' in *Gender and Development* Vol 3 no 1, Oxfam, Oxford.

Based on a paper presented to FINNIDA in Helsinki, 1989.

Molyneux, M 'Mobilisation without Emancipation? Women's Interests, States and Revolution in Nicaragua', *Feminist Studies* 11, 2, 1985.

In this paper, Maxine Molyneux develops the idea of practical and strategic gender interests which was later adapted by Caroline Moser in the Moser Framework's use of practical and strategic gender needs.

Moser, C 'Gender Planning in the Third World: Meeting Women's Practical and Strategic Needs', *World Development*, Vol 17, No.11, 1989.

In this article, Caroline Moser outlined the Moser Framework.

Moser, Caroline *Gender Planning and Development. Theory, practice and Training*, Routledge, UK/ USA, 1993.

This is a key text for understanding the Moser Framework. It outlines the theory and practice her gender planning methods, and includes an appendix on the methodology and content of gender-planning training.

Overholt C, Anderson MB, Cloud K, and Austin JE (1985) *Gender Roles in Development Projects: A Case Book*, Kumarian Press, West Hartford, USA.

Used in training a number of international agencies such as the World Bank, the US agency for International Development (USAID), and the Canadian International Development Agency (CIDA), it is the basic theoretical tool for the Harvard method. The first section provides background reading in technical areas concerning women and development and introduces an overall framework for project analysis. The second section is case studies intended as a vehicle for group discussion.

Sen, G and Grown, C DAWN (1985) 'Development Crises & Alternative Visions', *Third World Women's Perspectives*, Earthscan.

Williams S with Seed J, and Mwau A (1995) *Oxfam Gender Training Manual*, Oxfam GB, Oxford.

Contains a wide variety of exercises to use in training on gender frameworks. Its sections include: key concepts, gender awareness, gender roles and needs, gender sensitive appraisal and planning, gender and global issues, working with women and men. An excellent and comprehensive collection of gender training exercises tried and tested over ten years of Oxfam's work on gender and development.

Appendix: The gender policy and planning programme (GPPP) at the Development Planning Unit (DPU), University College London

The following section describes how the tools of the Moser Framework (see chapter 2.3) have been adapted in the past 12 years. This introduction is based on DPU Gender Policy and Planning Training Materials (1997) and has been compiled with the help of Fra von Massow and Caren Levy.

The DPU's rationale for gender policy and planning

For planning purposes, the DPU recognise the need to disaggregate categories such as 'household', 'community', 'target group', and so on. It is also necessary to analyse the gender division of labour and to identify the different household structures which exist beyond the nuclear household.

In addition, the DPU recognise that women and men, and girls and boys have different gender roles and different access to and control over resources; therefore, they have different gender needs. These can be practical gender needs (PGNs) or strategic gender needs (SGNs). These are reflected in different policy approaches to development.

Gender roles

Moser defines gender as the socially constructed relations between women and men in a particular context. In her analysis, she concentrates on the 'triple role' of women (reproductive, productive, and community management). The DPU framework aims to understand the social, economic, and political relations between women and men to identify the 'multiple roles' of women and men. Men's gender roles are identified and included in the analysis.

The DPU framework replaces Moser's category of 'community politics' with that of 'constituency-based politics', in order to incorporate women's and men's activities not only at community level but also at the national and international levels. The constituency-based politics role is 'undertaken on behalf of interest-based constituencies, within traditional structures, party politics, and/ or lobbying/ campaigning groups' (DPU GPPP, 1997).

Resources

The DPU's methodology analyses women's and men's access to and control over resources in their reproductive, productive, community-managing, and constituency-based politics roles before identifying gender needs.

The analysis of resources (such as food, health-care, productive resources, information, and access to political structures) recognises that negotiating and decision-making processes reflect power relations between women and men. Women and girls often have unequal access in the distribution of resources, for consumption as well as production, within and outside the household.

Gender needs

In the DPU methodology, gender needs are identified following an analysis of roles and resources. Although Moser's definition (see pp 57-58) remains largely valid, the DPU's GPPP shows a significant shift towards identifying men's gender needs in the context of inequitable gender relations and women's subordination. The following are current DPU definitions:

Practical Gender Needs (PGNs): These are 'the needs identified by women and men which arise out of the customary gender division of labour. PGNs are a response to immediate perceived necessity, identified within a specific context. They are often concerned with inadequacies in living conditions such as water provision, health care, and employment' (DPU, GPPP Training Materials 1997 adapted from Molyneux, M. (1985) and Moser, C. (1993)).

Strategic Gender Needs (SGNs): These needs 'reflect a challenge to the customary gender relations and imply a change in relationships of power and control between women and men. Those SGNs which women identify arise from women's recognition of, and challenge to, their subordinate position in relation to men in their society; for example, regarding equal access to employment, equal pay, equal legal rights. Those SGNs which men identify arise from men's recognition of and challenge to their exclusion from certain domains imposed by customary male roles, which contribute to the perpetuation of women's subordination, for example, sharing childcare. SGNs are context-specific' (DPU, GPPP Training Materials 1997 adapted from Molyneux, M. (1985) and Moser, C. (1993)).

Policy approaches to development, women, and gender

This tool helps to analyse the intention behind development interventions. It diagnoses the degree to which institutions reflect and promote gender equality both internally and in their work. It does so by identifying both 'explicit' and 'implicit' policy towards women/ gender. The tool also helps its users differentiate between the intentions of various macro-level policy approaches and their actual impact on women and men, girls and boys.

The DPU has identified ten different policy approaches, each categorised in terms of which gender roles and resources they focus on and which gender needs they meet. The categories also list in what climate of prevalent political and economic thought the various policy approaches have mainly been used.

- the pre-WID welfare approach (1940s-60s) under accelerated economic growth;

- the WID equity approach and

- the WID anti-poverty approach (1970s) under distribution with growth and basic-needs policies;

- the WID efficiency approach (1980s/90s) under structural adjustment and economic efficiency measures;

- the emancipation approach (1940-1989) under state socialist development;

- the empowerment approach (1970s onwards) under the New International Economic Order;

- the GAD integration approach (1980s/90s) under social sustainability with economic and political reform.

More recently, the DPU has added the following policy approaches to gender which reflect the changed policy climate in the 1990s.

- the GAD efficiency approach;

- the GAD equity approach; and

- the GAD anti-poverty approach, under social sustainability with economic adjustment and political reform. This approach aims to alleviate poverty while increasing production and employment.

The web of institutionalisation

The 'web of institutionalisation' is the central tool in the DPU's gender policy and planning methodology. This is a tool developed by Caren Levy based on the DPU's work with practitioners and activists at local, national, and international levels (Levy, C. 1996). The 'web' is used to assess how the gender perspective is currently institutionalised in a particular context. It identifies at least 13 elements which are crucial to the process of institutionalisation. Each element represents a 'site of power' of social relations, and the elements relate to each other in a set of reinforcing triangles, which make up the web (see

Figure 3). The various elements are outlined below. Each element, and its relation to other elements, is diagnosed using the adaptation of Moser's and Molyneux's concepts: the analysis of gender roles, resources, and policy approaches provide a basic language for carrying out the web diagnosis.

Based on these concepts, the diagnosis of the web identifies problems (i.e., weak or no gender integration) and potentials (to integrate gender). The final step in the preliminary gender diagnosis is to prioritise the problems and potentials, and to clarify starting points for action. Thus, gender diagnosis is an initial component of the DPU's gender policy and planning process.

The elements in the web of institutionalisation

There is no sequence for applying the web in practice: one can start anywhere. This example of the web begins with women and men in 'communities'[11] themselves. The first element in this example is *women's and men's experience and interpretation of reality* (rather than that of outside planners).

In order to achieve sustainable change, women's and men's experience must be expressed through collective action in the political arena. Through raising awareness and mobilisation, women and men can initiate collective action on particular gender interests, forming new political constituencies or joining existing ones, thus creating *pressure of political constituencies*. People face a range of gender, class, age, or ethnic constraints, as well as opportunities, which will shape such action (see Moser 1989).

In addition, women and men must be able to elect and/ or actively engage with *representative political structures* within the formal political system; otherwise, their interests will remain outside formal politics. 'Representative' here means that the profile of the representatives in terms of gender, ethnicity, and so on reflects the profile of a population in a given context. It also means that the representatives reflect the practical and strategic gender interests of the women and men they represent.

The three elements outlined above reinforce each other (see Figure 1); this is critical for sustained change.

Pressure of political constituencies and representative political structures needs to be supported by *political commitment*: the public articulation of a political intent or stand. This sets the tone for action, which others either

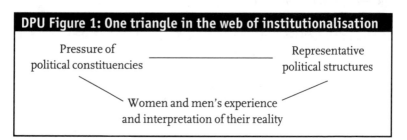

DPU Figure 1: One triangle in the web of institutionalisation

Pressure of political constituencies ──────────── Representative political structures

Women and men's experience and interpretation of their reality

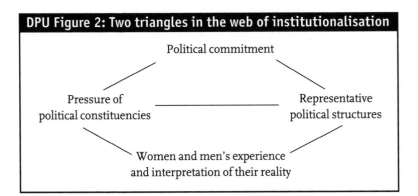

DPU Figure 2: Two triangles in the web of institutionalisation

Political commitment

Pressure of political constituencies

Representative political structures

Women and men's experience and interpretation of their reality

support or oppose. Thus, the initial triangle overlaps with a second triangle of elements (see Figure 2 above). The resulting web diagram can be 'read' to see the way in which the various elements reinforce each other.

Figure 3 shows the relationships between various triangles, and includes further elements of the web, which are explained in the following.

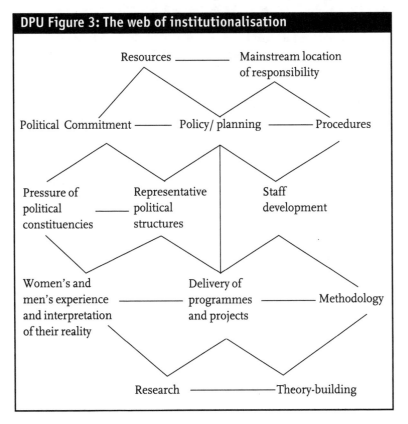

DPU Figure 3: The web of institutionalisation

Resources — Mainstream location of responsibility

Political Commitment — Policy/ planning — Procedures

Pressure of political constituencies

Representative political structures

Staff development

Women's and men's experience and interpretation of their reality

Delivery of programmes and projects — Methodology

Research — Theory-building

The test of *political commitment* is whether it is translated into *policy* and *resources*. In the web, neither integrated policies or separate policies are seen as enough by themselves: resources support policy. All too often, the financial support allocated to gender policy is minuscule compared to budgets for other policy areas. Gender integration implies the use of existing policy and programmes, but in a gender-aware way. Nevertheless, new and current resources to promote and maintain this kind of integration are critical. For example, a budget might be created for training and demonstration projects.

The allocation of resources and the creation and enactment of policy depend fundamentally on the *mainstream location of responsibility* for gender issues. An gender-aware approach such as WID/ GAD can easily be marginalised if a specific institution is created for it. All associated institutions must be given responsibility for integrating gender concerns into their remit. Integration must not be left to the WID/ GAD department or ministry.

Responsibility for gender issues in the institution, including adherence to gender policies, must be reinforced by gendered *procedures* (routine daily activities and documents, such as terms of reference). Again, it is not sufficient to have WID/GAD procedures in isolation from the 'mainstream' procedures of the institution. Mainstream procedures must be made gender-aware, and this again must be seen as the responsibility of each part of an organisation or institution. Gender-blind procedures can quickly undermine individual commitment or gender-aware policies.

This analysis leads to a central triangle in the web, which links *policy*, *procedures*, and *staff development*. Both policy and procedures will be limited without the appropriate staff development, including training in gender policy and planning for both women and men, as well as equal opportunities in recruitment, access to training, promotion, and so on. Effective staff development requires a clear *methodology*; that is, a methodology which has a clear rationale for integrating gender into development practice as well as tools for applying this in the work of practitioners. Policy, procedures and training for staff reinforce each other – training on its own does not change practice in a sustained way. Because of existing gender power relations, gender training in the absence of clear gendered policies and procedures is a waste of time.

Another aspect of staff development is the progress of women and men workers through their organisation; this depends mainly on the working conditions in the organisation. Again, it seems to be the case that both separate and integrated affirmative action is required, rather than one or the other.

However, if staff development and appropriate methodology do not result in the actual *'delivery' of programmes and projects*[12] which meet the needs of women and men, then programmes and projects are unsuccessful, and the institutionalisation of gender has failed. This element is a pivotal point linked to a number of reinforcing triangles in the web – see Figure 3. For instance, a supportive policy environment is critical for good 'delivery'.

For effective institutionalisation of gender issues in development organisations, not only professionals and practitioners must be involved, but also women and men from the communities the organisation works with. Furthermore, if programmes and projects are to relate to women and men's experience and their interpretation of reality, their interests and needs must be reflected in making decisions through their active involvement in representative political structures. These would include structures at all levels: the national, the local, and the programme level.

Effective 'delivery' must respond to changes in women's and men's experience, and to the way in which they interpret such change. Applied *research* can be a critical reinforcing element here. For example, gender-sensitive participatory-research techniques can empower men and women in communities and promote the 'ownership' of activities, as well as act as monitoring and feedback mechanisms to improve programmes and projects.

Finally, applied research contributes to a body of knowledge about the integration of gender issues in the practice of policy and planning. It adds to *theory-building* on gender and the development of methodology. Furthermore, methodology reinforces not only research but also practice, and strengthens the education of the next generation of practitioners and researchers.

Gender mainstreaming in practice

Recognising both the resistance and opportunities to gender integration which emerge from particular power relations in specific contexts, the DPU's framework puts forward a gender policy and planning process which is an iterative, rather than a linear, process.

While carrying out gender diagnosis using the web of institutionalisation is an initiating part of this process, diagnosis is a continuous process and constantly interacts with another component of the gender policy and planning process: gender consultation. Using a variety of methods, gender consultation involves dialogue with the women and men of a community to define their own gender needs, as well as dialogue and advocacy with women and men involved in organisations working in a particular context. Problems, potentials, and prioritisation of goals are refined during this consultation.

On the basis of the gender diagnosis and gender consultation, entry points for action are identified by developing working objectives and entry strategies. These widen the opportunities for integrating gender issues through putting the process of gender diagnosis and gender consultation into practice. Two further components of the gender policy and planning process are organisational development and monitoring and impact assessment. These four components are iteratively linked, and continuously interact.Thus the gender policy and planning process develops alongside organisational ways of working to institutionalise or 'mainstream' a gender perspective in development practice.

References

DPU Gender Policy and Planning Programme Training Materials, 1997

Levy, C. 1996 The Institutionalisation of Gender Policy and Planning, The Web of Institutionalisation, DPU Working Paper No 74

DPU News 1998

Notes

1 This definition is intended to contain the notion of sustainability in the changes brought to the practices of formal institutions, in other words it encompasses the idea of institutionalisation (Levy 1996). Thus the two terms (institutionalisation and mainstreaming) remain distinguishable by the emphasis that 'institutionalisation' puts on the sustainability of changes, though for some the two are synonymous (Byme and Laier 1996).

2 This definition is the one Caren Levy offers for 'tools' (Levy 1996, 4).

3 'Gender' has been used in this sense in Europe and North America for about the past 25 years, since the publication of Ann Oakley's book Sex and Gender in 1971. Prior to this, 'gender' was only used in its other, older, meaning of a grammatical term used in the study of language. Many dictionaries still limit themselves to including only this definition.

4 Maxine Molyneux first coined the distinction between the terms 'practical' and 'strategic' using the concept of gender interests. Caroline Moser then adapted this distinction for planning, using the concept of gender needs. These different terms signify a difference in approach. The term 'needs' has been criticised as suggesting that women are passive recipients of assistance determined by external planners. In contrast, 'interests' is a more active concept, because it implies that women themselves define their demands. (Kabeer 1994).

5 This case study is a synopsis of a much longer case-study in Kabeer 1994, p273. Kabeer illustrates her point by examining a case study from Anne-Marie Goetz's 1989 paper titled 'Misbehaving Policy: A Feminist Analysis of Assumptions Informing a Project for Women Fish-smokers in Guinea', presented at the Canadian Association of Africa Scholars' Annual Meeting, Queen's College, Kingston, Ontario.

6 Note, here a third category of activities (socio-political) has been added to the

Harvard Analytical Framework, as an adaptation of Moser's (1986) triple role concept.

7 See Kabeer 1994, p 277, for further discussion.

8 Rani Parker developed the GAM when she was on staff at Save the Children Federation and wrote it during her employment at The Salvation Army World Service Office. She is now an independent consultant on gender and development.

9 This case study is based on a trip to Chile by Candida March undertaken for Oxfam in March 1992.

10 The Logical Framework 'is a tool to aid project (and programme) planning and management, especially management at strategic and institutional level' (Wiggins S and Shields D 'Logical Framework' in *Project Appraisal* vol 10 no1 March 1995, pp 2-12).

11 Community is used here not as an undifferentiated unit, but with the recognition of the heterogeneity and diversity of communities on the basis of class, ethnicity, religion, age as well as gender.

12 'Delivery' is put in quotation marks, as the term might imply a top-down activity and this is not the intention.

Index